Foodservice
Management
Professional® (FMP®)

Certification Examination
Review Manual

NATIONAL
RESTAURANT
ASSOCIATION®

Disclaimer

Table of Contents
FMP Review Manual

Preface

This edition of the *Foodservice Management Professional® (FMP®) Certification Examination Review Manual* incorporates the following features:

□ Introduction has been expanded to include instructions on how to prepare for the examination.

□ More practice test items, grouped by the subject matter that the participant is likely to encounter on the actual examination.

□ Specific performance-based objectives matched to the review questions.

□ Additional study references for publications available through the National Restaurant Association.

Introduction

The purpose of this manual is to help you prepare to take the two-section FMP certification examination. You may choose to study and take each one individually or both in the same session. The organization of this manual gives you the flexibility to study the areas you deem necessary to meet your examination preparation objectives.

I. Organization of the Manual

The manual consists of five chapters, one covering each of the following topics:

□ Operations Management

□ Risk Management

□ Human Resources Management

□ Unit Revenue and Cost Management

□ Marketing Management

Each chapter is divided into sub-categories and in some cases, further divided into subject topics within these categories. Each subject topic has the following instructional elements:

□ Brief introduction to the subject topic highlighting the importance of the topic to the foodservice industry.

□ Learning objectives that correlate to the review questions at the end of the chapter.

□ Additional references for study for materials offered by the National Restaurant Association.

□ Summary information for important topics; however, this manual is not a substitute for more detailed and extensive study of the subjects in the examination.

□ Review questions at the end of each chapter.

II. How to Use this Manual

Before you begin to study, determine whether you will take both sections of the examination at the same time or take each individually. Once you have decided, it is recommended you use the following effective and efficient method of study.

Concentrate on one chapter at a time. Complete the cycle of study, test, and review for each chapter. Study the relevant chapter, focusing on the learning objectives, topic discussions, exhibits, and perhaps reference other sources of information. You are now ready to answer the end-of-chapter review questions.

It is important to practice the end-of-chapter review questions as though they are the actual test. Do not refer to the book for answers while practicing. After all, you are trying to gauge how prepared you are for the actual certification examination. (Calculators are permitted.)

Score the test by comparing your results against the answer key. The review questions are organized by subject topic so you can easily reference the correct answers to questions you may have answered incorrectly. Keep in mind that these items are not the actual examination questions. It is important to study the whole section or chapter of the materials found in the References section. Many of the books referenced also include test items which you may also choose to review. You will enhance your knowledge on the subject and gain additional practice in answering test items.

Some applicants may be involved in a special review class to prepare to take the two-section FMP examination. Your instructor may be a valuable resource to either explain the answers to the questions or help you locate the appropriate resource material. FMP examination candidates are also encouraged to form study groups.

III. Examination-Taking Tips

Here are some specific tips that will aid you in taking the examinations:

☐ Within each group of questions, the easier questions are usually at the beginning of the group and the more difficult ones are at the end. If you are working on a group of questions of a particular type and find that the questions are getting too difficult for you, read through the rest of the questions in that group and answer only those you think you know. Then continue on to the next group of questions.

☐ After you have answered all the questions about which you feel confident, go back and answer the items you skipped. One reliable approach to answering multiple-choice questions is to rule out responses that you know to be wrong and then make your best guess at the correct answer from the remaining alternatives.

☐ Make sure you answer every question. There is no penalty for incorrectly answering a question (i.e., no points are deducted from your score for an incorrect answer).

IV. For more information on the FMP program:

Call:
800.765.2122, ext. 6703
In Chicagoland 312.715.1010, ext. 6703

Email:
certification@restaurant.org

Visit our Web site:
www.restaurant.org

Write:
National Restaurant Association
Exam Administration
175 W. Jackson Blvd., Suite 1500
Chicago, Illinois 60604-2814

References

As you work through this manual, you will see that every major topic will contain references to other, more detailed treatments of the respective topics. As noted in the Introduction, the instructional material in the manual is of a summary nature and is not intended to replace the standard course instruction for these topics. If you are unfamiliar with or need to review any of the topics in this manual, you should pursue a more in-depth study of those subjects by referring to the informational and instructional sources listed at the end of each chapter. The references show the complete title, authorship, copyright date, and publisher.

The National Restaurant Association offers a variety of materials you may find useful for review.

For more information on the National Restaurant Association's products call 800.765.2122 or in Chicagoland 312.715.1010, ext. 6701, or visit our Web site at www.restaurant.org.

Chapter 1 Outline

I. Customer Service
- A. Setting Service Standards
- B. Providing Good Service
  1. Taking Reservations
  2. Customer Arrival
  3. Well-Trained Employees
  4. Serving Customers with Special Needs
- C. Handling Complaints
- D. Customer Feedback

II. Menu Planning and Management
- A. Menu Development
- B. Establishing Prices
  1. Pricing Based on Costs
  2. Pricing Factor or Multiplier
  3. Variable Cost Pricing
  4. Prime Cost Pricing
  5. Combined Food and Labor Costs
  6. Actual Cost Pricing
  7. Gross Profit Pricing
  8. One Price Method
  9. Cost-Plus-Profit Pricing
  10. Minimum Charge Pricing
- C. Evaluating Pricing
- D. Menu Analysis
- E. Providing Nutritious Menu Items

III. Responsible Alcohol Service
- A. Legal Liability
- B. Responsible Policies
- C. Responsible Promotions
- D. Incident Reports

IV. Food Quality
- A. Controlling Production Quantities
- B. Controlling Production Standards

V. Inventory Functions
- A. Purchasing Food and Beverages
  1. Selecting a Supplier
  2. Purchase Specifications
- B. Receiving Food and Beverages
- C. Maintaining Inventory
- D. Issuing Food and Beverages from Inventory

VI. Facility Maintenance
- A. Maintaining Facilities
  1. Selecting Equipment
  2. Maintaining Equipment

VII. Review Questions

Chapter 1
Operations Management

Learning Objectives

You will be asked to:

☆ Define the function of a mission statement.

☆ Recognize why servers should have thorough product knowledge.

☆ State how to help customers with special needs.

☆ Identify the most efficient way to record customer reservations.

☆ Describe appropriate service behaviors.

☆ Outline methods of asking customers about the quality of their food and service.

☆ Explain the steps in resolving customer complaints to their satisfaction.

☆ Recommend the best response when receiving complaints from angry customers.

☆ Discuss the best course of action when confronted with a persistent complaint.

Customer Service

More than anything else, the level and quality of service distinguishes one operation from another. Quality service is based on attention to details, efficiency, consistency, and professionalism.

Setting Service Standards

A *mission statement* defines an operation's goals and directs both managers and employees toward the goal of satisfying customers. When properly identified and applied, a mission statement gives a business focus and profoundly affects its success. A mission statement should:

☐ Distinguish the food.

☐ Define the service.

☐ Identify the atmosphere.

☐ Define the price range.

☐ State how the operation distinguishes itself from the competition.

All foodservice customers expect proper service. Delivering good customer service is by far the most challenging responsibility of foodservice managers. Reports have shown that the majority of people who do not return to a foodservice operation were dissatisfied with the service, not the food. After all, when people simply want food, they can stay at home.

To provide good service, management must set high *service standards,* communicate them to employees, see that they are met or exceeded, and support employees in their effort through training and recognition. Standards are specific rules, principles, or measures established to guide employees in performing their duties consistently. Service standards include service policies and service mechanics models such as how to pour water, deliver food to the table, service guests over the counter, set up a table, or prepare a service station. Management establishes service standards based on the type of operation and the quality of service it wants to achieve. Standards vary from the elegant service required in a fine-dining establishment to that appropriate for casual facilities, on-site operations, and even quick-service operations.

Excellent customer service cannot occur by chance; it is the result of sound planning and management. A manager of excellent customer service must identify problems and their causes, set goals, consider available resources, develop policies and procedures, and obtain feedback and monitor results.

Providing Good Service

Employee indifference is the easiest way to turn customers away from your business and towards the competition. This directly influences sales and profits—it costs five times more to attract a new customer than it does to keep a steady one. Customers get an overall impression of an operation from its employees. Every time a customer comes in contact with an employee—or the work performed by an employee—an opportunity exists to win that customer for life. A satisfied customer is your greatest asset, returning again and again, bringing friends, and telling others about your excellent service. A customer is a lifetime investment and not easily replaced. So, it is important that employees are well trained in providing the level and quality of service appropriate to your establishment.

Taking Reservations

Typically, reservations are accepted by full-service operations. Quick-service managers, however, should understand the process and procedures associated with handling reservations effectively. Even though an employee or server may handle reservations, it is ultimately the manager's responsibility for establishing the reservation system and monitoring its operation. The person who takes the reservation provides the first impression of the operation, so a courteous attitude is key. Reservations should be arranged to achieve the best possible turnover while still providing exceptional service. Usually a dinner table of one or two people will remain occupied

for an hour and a half, though breakfast and lunch tables turnover much faster. Staggering reservations prevents a crowd of people coming in all at one time and avoids overloading both your kitchen and service staff.

A manager may want to reconsider accepting reservations if no-shows or cancellations become a problem. If an establishment has enough walk-in business to be successful, reservation systems may be a burden rather than a help.

Customer Arrival

The outside of a foodservice establishment should be inviting. The grounds should be clean, well-lit, and secure. When entering a foodservice operation, there should be an overall impression that is consistent with the mission statement. The color, sound, lighting, and décor should be pleasing and give guests a positive feeling. The air conditioning, heating, and ventilation should be comfortable.

Well-Trained Employees

Successful service staff have a professional appearance with a positive, helpful, and courteous demeanor and possess a high level of knowledge of food and service. Professional servers can accommodate guests who have a variety of needs from special dietary requirements to a clear understanding of laws and regulations that directly affect food service.

The best way to guarantee that all guests receive consistently good service is to communicate a service commitment to every employee in the organization. Every employee is crucial, whether or not he or she regularly sees customers. Those who have direct contact with customers need to be aware of how important their impression is to customers' perception of the operation. A professional appearance, positive attitude, sincerity, honesty, and courtesy are all essential in making a positive impression.

In addition, employees who have little direct customer contact need to support front-line employees who serve as their internal customers.

Employees should be encouraged to anticipate not only their customers' needs, but coworkers' needs as well, as teamwork is crucial in delivering outstanding customer service. Service staff need to have a good relationship with kitchen staff so that orders are filled accurately and promptly. Communication among employees needs to be clear and effective at all times. Service staff need to know the role other employees play in accomplishing food production and service.

Because employees are so important to retaining customers, make sure they are adequately trained in the following aspects of good service.

☐ **Focus completely on the customer.** Greet customers warmly and sincerely the minute they walk through the door. When they leave, customers deserve to be thanked and bid goodbye. Ensure prompt, friendly, courteous service from the moment customers arrive at your establishment to the moment they walk out the door.

☐ **Show a sense of urgency.** Demonstrate to your customers that their needs are important. Responding immediately to a customer's special request lets them know that they are your number-one priority.

☐ **Behave consistently despite unusual or unexpected circumstances.** Even when a dozen things go wrong, keep a positive attitude and a friendly demeanor.

☐ **Try to anticipate and accommodate the customers' needs.** Watch and listen to customers carefully for clues to what their needs might be, do whatever you think is necessary to please customers, and think creatively when serving customers.

☐ **Know the signs of a dissatisfied customer and respond immediately and appropriately.** When customers do not receive a basic level of service, they will be disappointed, irritated, annoyed, or even angry.

☐ **Have thorough knowledge of the menu.** All service staff should know preparation techniques for all menu items, their ingredients, and their approximate preparation times. Service staff should know daily specials as well as current promotions. They should also be aware of any unavailable items.

☐ **Work efficiently.** Learn to plan and organize to make the best use of time.

☐ **Practice good timing.** Customers want to be served at their own pace. In general, a course should not be served within five minutes after the preceding one is finished. Another course should not be served until customers are through with the previous one. Do not rush customers who want to linger.

☐ **Clear dirty dishes from the table promptly.** Always clear away dirty dishes before placing full dishes in front of customers and never allow customers to sit at dirty tables.

Do everything that you can to make customers' experience in your establishment as pleasant as possible.

Ultimately, it is the manager who is responsible for good service. Employees who are poorly trained, unhappy in their jobs, treated harshly by their supervisors, or not provided with the proper supplies and support will not deliver good service. Successful managers should invest in thorough employee training, expect the best performance from their employees, reward desired employee behavior, and treat employees with the respect and courtesy they are expected to show customers.

Serving Customers with Special Needs

Always be respectful when accommodating customers with special needs. Help customers who might have difficulty hearing, walking, or carrying food to a table, or must count money slowly. When serving families with children, know about any special children's menu items and where to find children's seats. Food allergies can be severe and, on occasion, fatal. It is imperative that all servers know the exact ingredients in every menu item.

Customers using crutches, canes, and walkers may have them stored near their table, but not in the way of other customers. People in wheelchairs may need their chair removed for them, or assistance from their wheelchair to their chair at the table. Customers with disabilities affecting their hands or arms may require special utensils.

When serving customers with hearing or speech impairments, staff should speak clearly, use a notepad, or point to items on the menu for clarification. Vision-impaired customers may need to be assisted to their table and have the menu described to them. Guide dogs should stay near the table where they can see their owner. When presenting the check to sight-impaired customers, the server should clearly state the individual prices as well as the total.

Handling Complaints

In spite of your best efforts, there will be occasions when things go wrong and a customer is unhappy. Plan ahead for possible problems. Have clear-cut lines of authority worked out with your employees, and train them to be professional in every situation. They should be trained to:

☐ Stay calm.

☐ Listen carefully.

☐ Empathize.

☐ Avoid becoming defensive.

☐ Accept responsibility.

☐ Work to find a solution.

☐ Follow up with the customer or another employee to be sure the customer is satisfied with the solution.

It is much easier to prevent problems than to fix them once a customer becomes unhappy. The best way to prevent most complaints is to ensure that all jobs are done with care.

Employees should notify the manager of all complaints, even if a complaint has already been resolved. If possible, the manager should apologize personally or with a written note to customers who have complained and assure them that the problem was handled correctly. Customers appreciate a manager who is genuinely concerned about them. However, a manager should never criticize a member of the staff when apologizing to a customer.

When receiving complaints from angry customers, be sure to listen fully to their explanation of the problem. Make sure that all customer complaints are resolved promptly. Customers who complain are not troublemakers; they help you find and correct problems. Statistics show that a customer whose complaint is handled will remain your customer.

Customer Feedback

An operation should take an active interest in encouraging customer feedback to improve the quality of service it provides. Receiving feedback from customers is one important way to monitor results of a service plan and maintain high standards.

It is important that service staff be sincere when they stop at the table after the food has been served to inquire how the meal is going. If possible, a manager might make rounds—"table visits"— periodically to ensure that customers are satisfied. The cashier might also invite the customer to share any comments about the service.

Many establishments use comment cards to invite customer feedback. Comment cards should be simple enough so that they are not an imposition for customers, who, after all, are not looking for work to do when they eat out. General results should be tabulated and circulated so that every manager and employee is aware of them. Praise employees who are complimented and instruct employees about whom you receive complaints on how they can improve their service. All problems revealed by the comment cards should be taken seriously and corrected immediately.

Mystery shoppers provide more in-depth feedback than can be obtained on comment cards. Mystery shoppers are hired to visit an operation and report on their experiences. They are usually trained so that they know standards, systems, and procedures particular to an operation and can comment specifically on them. This type of program should be introduced in a positive way, as an opportunity for everyone to see how customers view them.

Other ways of obtaining customer feedback include surveys and focus groups. Surveys should include specific rather than general questions. A focus group is a group of customers or employees called together regularly to brainstorm with you on how you can improve customer service. Especially when conducting focus groups involving employees, participants should feel free to say anything about the operation without fear of angering the management, and with the assurance that no one will repeat outside the meeting anything that was said inside.

Service has become the single most influential factor in customers' decisions when eating out. Great service gives operations a competitive edge and keeps people coming back.

References

1. *Presenting Service: The Ultimate Guide for the Foodservice Professional* by Lendal H. Kotschevar, FMP and Valentino Luciani ©1996 The Educational Foundation of the National Restaurant Association

You will be asked to:

☆ Choose menu items and a menu type consistent with a given mission statement of an establishment.

☆ Identify common types of menus.

☆ Distinguish between an effective menu design and a poor menu design.

☆ Describe factors that influence menu development.

☆ Explain the term yield analysis.

☆ State factors that influence pricing.

☆ List the methods for determining portion size and categorize specific food items by those methods.

☆ Estimate the selling price of a particular food item given its cost and the sales to cost ratio.

☆ Discuss methods of analyzing the success or failure of menu items.

☆ Outline the considerations an establishment must make when providing nutritious menu items to its clientele.

Menu Planning and Management

The menu is much more than a list of foods that patrons look at to choose meals. It represents the concept or the image that the operation is trying to convey and is a major marketing tool. Both commercial and noncommercial establishments develop menus to control costs, facilitate overall objectives of the institution, and provide operational efficiency.

Menu Development

The menu is the essential document for successful operation of the establishment. Menu planners must know the operation and potential market. They must know how the operational constraints, such as costs, equipment, and skills of labor affect the menu selection. Menu planning requires time and skill and is the most critical step in defining a foodservice operation. The menu defines the purpose, strategy, market, service, and theme of the operation.

There are a number of different menu types. The type of operation, intended customers, the type or number of meals served, and special occasions will help dictate the menu that will be successful in a particular foodservice facility. Many operations use special menus for breakfast, brunch, holidays, parties, and formal dinners. The major menu types include:

☐ A la carte, on which food items are listed and priced separately.

☐ Table d'hôte, on which groups of items are offered at a single price.

☐ Du jour, or daily menu.

☐ Limited, used in quick-service which offer only a few selected items.

☐ Cycle, food items are repeated after a set number of days or weeks.

☐ California, which lists items that are available at all times daily.

A number of factors both inside and outside the foodservice operator's control must be considered in menu development. These include:

☐ Physical layout of the facility, including space for storage, preparation, and service areas.

☐ Skill level and number of employees.

☐ Food quality and availability.

☐ Nutritional, physiological, social, and psychological needs of customers.

☐ Guest expectations regarding the menu offerings and prices.

☐ Food appeal, or the combined factors (appearance, temperature, texture, consistency, flavor) that make food items on a menu appealing to patrons.

☐ Profit margin.

These factors are important not only in planning food menu, but in planning liquor menus and wine lists.

The design of the menu establishes an identity and distinguishes your establishment from the competition. Different typeface styles can be used to portray certain settings or to emphasize particular food items. Generally, typefaces that have plain, sharp, crisp lettering are more legible than flowing type with a lot of adornment. Proper layout of food items and creative use of color will enhance a menu's eye appeal. A good menu will "grab" patrons and attract them to items the operation wants to sell. A menu that is clearly and attractively presented will sell more than one that is unappealing or ill-designed.

Many operations today print their own menus. Having personal control of menu production offers advantages such as reduced printing costs and increased flexibility. Among professional printers, certain companies specialize in assisting foodservice establishments to plan, develop, and print menus. They can be extremely helpful in producing an effective menu. Their experience in setting up menus can be helpful in avoiding mistakes.

Standard portion size, the fixed quantity served to a customer for a fixed selling price, is one of the most important standards an establishment sets. Menu items can be portioned by weight (meats, vegetables), volume (soups, beverages), and count (whole potatoes, asparagus spears). For some food items, particularly meat, the simple formula for determining standard portion size is replaced by a yield analysis. Processing must take place and inedible parts must be discarded before the yield, or number of usable portions produced, can be ascertained. The yield factor is the percentage of a total piece of meat available for portioning. To control liquor portions, many operations standardize their glassware in addition to measuring volume.

Standardized portion sizes, as well as standardized recipes, provide the necessary information to determine standard portion costs. These planned portion costs can be calculated for each menu item. To determine a standard portion cost, simply divide the cost of an item by the number of portions it contains. For example, croissants purchased at $4.50 for a box of fifteen cost $0.30 each. Once standard portion costs are established, the process of pricing menu items can begin.

Establishing Prices

Establishing and adjusting the prices of food and beverage items can be a complex task. There are a number of factors to consider when pricing menu items, including the market, the type of operation, and costs. The market is a major factor in pricing. Some patrons will want only low prices while others are willing to pay higher ones. Many operators use a "what the market will bear" approach to pricing. However, such a simplistic strategy may not meet operational needs and may drive patrons to competitors.

Menu prices must not only cover the costs of food and labor but must often include other significant cost factors such as atmosphere, rent—especially in a prime location—and advertising. Prices and price adjustments can be based on cost, sales potential, or promotional considerations. External factors such as elasticity of demand (whether a price change will alter demand) and competition must also be considered when adjusting prices. Finally, the type of foodservice operation and its organizational objectives will influence how the operation prices its menu. A for-profit luxury hotel restaurant will likely have different pricing objectives than an employer-subsidized cafeteria. Most operations use a combination of pricing methods to best meet their needs.

Pricing Based on Costs

There are a variety of pricing methods, but any organization's pricing method should be based on costs, not on simple instinct. For example, an operation begins its pricing adjustments by projecting its costs and revenue for the upcoming period. To find the desired cost percentage, they divide the projected costs by the projected food sales. This percentage is then used to price items. For example, if monthly food costs are projected to be $18,000 and monthly food sales are projected to be $62,000, then the food cost percentage is:

Food cost percentage = $18,000 ÷ Food sales

$62,000 = 0.290, or 29%

Based on this figure, if a menu item costs $1.12, then its selling price is $3.86.

Food cost ÷ Food cost percentage = Selling price

$1.12 ÷ 0.29% = $3.86

The selling price of $3.86 can then be rounded to an appropriate menu price.

In another pricing method, total revenue is divided by the number of seats, average seat turnover, and days open in one year to determine the average check needed. (To determine average cover, divide the day's total sales by the number of customers served. To determine the average seat turnover rate, divide the number of average daily customers by the number of seats in the operation.) This helps give an idea of the price range of menu items. This range, along with an approximate food cost percentage, can be used to determine each item's selling price.

Pricing Factor or Multiplier

A desired food cost percentage converts into a pricing factor or multiplier. The desired food cost percentage is multiplied to get a selling price. For example, a food's cost is $1.50, and the desired food percentage is 30 percent;

100% ÷ 30% = 3.33

and

3.33 × $1.50 = 4.995 ($5.00),

the selling price. If an operator wants a multiplier based on a combined food and labor cost, a multiplier can be calculated and used. An operator wants a multiplier based on a combined food and labor cost of 65 percent. The calculation is

100% ÷ 65% = 1.54.

If the combined food and labor cost were $4.20, the selling price would be

1.54 × $4.20 = $6.47, or $6.50.

Variable Cost Pricing

A *variable food cost pricing method* assigns levels of food cost markups for menu items. This method is used for à la carte menu and table d'hôte menu prices. Menu items are divided into high, medium, and low labor costs. This method weighs food cost and allows price to reflect the influence of labor as a cost.

Prime Cost Pricing

Prime cost is raw food cost plus *direct labor,* or labor spent in preparation. Direct labor figures can be obtained by timing work. If a food item cost $2.00 and the direct labor is $0.50, prime cost is $2.50. An operation that wants a 30 percent food cost and a 10 percent direct labor cost has a prime cost percentage of 40 percent.

Combined Food and Labor Costs

Prices can be based on a combination of food and labor percentages. If food cost for an item is $1.50 and labor is $1.00, then the selling price ($1.50 + $1.00) is $2.50.

Actual Cost Pricing

Some pricing methods are based on actual costs for each menu item according to employee preparation, supplier price systems, and indirect operating costs. Costs are divided into food, labor, and operating cost units. This method is useful only in conjunction with an accurate and proficient cost accounting system.

Gross Profit Pricing

In gross profit pricing, the gross profit dollar figure is taken from the profit and loss statement for a certain period. This is divided by the number of guests served during the time to get an average dollar gross profit per guest.

One Price Method

If the overall cost of menu items is generally the same, such as it would be at a gourmet coffee shop, the operation can charge just one or a few prices to simplify things.

Cost-Plus-Profit Pricing

Some pricing methods calculate profits directly into the menu item prices. For instance, a standard amount of profit is set for each patron. The food, labor, and operating costs are added together, and then the desired profit is added. This covers all the costs and should result in a desired profit. Next, an average labor cost plus value and operating cost value are determined from the profit and loss statement, and both are divided by the number of patrons served in that period. This method tends to even out selling prices.

Minimum Charge Pricing

Every customer costs a certain amount to serve, and by having a minimum charge these costs will be covered. Pricing is set on a menu to make it impossible to obtain service below a certain price. Private clubs often require members to spend a specific amount on food during a certain time period.

Evaluating Pricing

Pricing is an ongoing process. Prices need to be evaluated constantly, based on adequate information, to study how customers react to prices, and to gather data on costs. Gathering, compiling, collating, and filing pricing data are as much a part of the pricing function as the establishment of prices.

Menu Analysis

Not only do prices need to be monitored and evaluated, but the actual items on a menu need evaluating as well. It is necessary to check often to see whether menu items are selling. Managers must ensure that information regarding the daily number of menu items sold is recorded accurately and completely. Items should be changed if they do not produce sales. The methods of analyzing menu items include:

☐ Keep a count of items sold per period.

☐ Conduct a subjective evaluation, in which management and others, such as skilled consultants, examine the menu.

☐ Develop a popularity index, in which item counts are analyzed in terms of percentage ratios to overall item sales.

☐ Create a menu factor analysis, in which the performance of menu items or groups of items can be judged on the basis of popularity, revenue, food cost, and gross profit margin.

☐ Evaluate the effectiveness of menu items toward total sales and profits using a goal value analysis.

A sales mix record shows the amount of each menu item sold over a specific period of time, and can be done daily, weekly, or monthly. By studying past sales mix records, a manager can see if a drop in an item's popularity is seasonal, caused by production problems, or poor server sales techniques. Those items that have a high sales volume are called leaders; items with a low sales volume are called losers.

Menu development is actually a continuous process, and most menu items and prices can never be considered final.

Providing Nutritious Menu Items

More and more Americans are making healthy changes in their eating habits. Interest in nutritious foods is no longer just for health food "types" or those on medically restricted diets. Though the science of nutrition continues to change, one fact remains the same—people must eat the right foods in the proper balance to be healthy. The goal of foodservice managers must be to offer a variety of healthful, appealing, and high-quality foods. A basic knowledge of nutrients and their sources helps foodservice managers to know how to meet the goal of preparing and serving healthful and appealing foods. The manager must also have knowledge of special, but often common, dietary needs. Examples are the needs of persons with diabetes, restricted sodium or low cholesterol diets, food allergies, or food intolerance.

When making menu changes, it is important to use nutrition guidelines that meet customers' perceived needs and that can be realistically implemented within the scope of the operation. Several factors should be considered, such as how nutrition-oriented the clientele is; whether customers are generally interested in healthy, fresh food or about losing weight or preventing heart attacks; and the present menu style and how existing menu items can be adapted within the limits of the kitchen staff. Formal or informal in-house market research is very helpful in answering such questions.

One relatively safe way to introduce change is to choose existing dishes that are particularly nutritious and identify them as such on the menu. Then, choose a few other dishes that are familiar to your customers and modify them slightly. Next, develop new dishes. Remember that the more closely new healthy alternatives resemble current menu items in quality, taste, appearance, and price, the more readily they will be accepted by customers. If the first attempts at healthier fare are popular, they may draw customers back. If patrons frequent the restaurant regularly, such as in hospital and employee cafeterias, healthful alternatives can be changed daily to provide variety. Many restaurant menus meet all the criteria for healthy eating by using absolutely fresh ingredients and uncomplicated preparations. Standard ways of making recipes more healthful involve deleting ingredients, substituting ingredients, or changing cooking techniques.

References

1. *Management by Menu, Third Edition* by Lendal H. Kotschevar, FMP and Marcel R. Escoffier ©1994 The Educational Foundation of the National Restaurant Association

2. *Nutrition for the Foodservice Professional, Third Edition* by Karen Eich Drummond, FMP ©1997 John Wiley and Sons, Inc.

3. *Presenting Service: The Ultimate Guide for the Foodservice Professional* by Lendal H. Kotschevar, FMP and Valentino Luciani ©1996 The Educational Foundation of the National Restaurant Association

Learning Objectives

You will be asked to:

☆ Choose the most effective way for a server to monitor excessive drinking by patrons.

☆ Recognize the signs of intoxication.

☆ Define third-party liability.

☆ Identify who can be refused liquor service.

☆ Outline the elements of a responsible alcohol service program.

☆ Determine potential liability in a drunken driving situation.

☆ Modify an ineffective responsible alcohol service training program.

☆ Explain how to thoroughly complete an alcohol-related incident report.

Responsible Alcohol Service

Legal Liability

Serving beverage alcohol responsibly means helping customers enjoy beverage alcohol's pleasant aspects while safeguarding them from the unpleasant and possibly dangerous effects of drinking too much. Liability for liquor service is one of the most serious issues confronting foodservice operators today. Operators licensed to sell alcohol have responsibilities that go beyond buying good liquor and hiring a bartender to fix drinks.

The liquor code is the body of legal statutes that governs your liquor license. Under the code, it is illegal to serve alcohol to minors, intoxicated persons, and known or habitual alcoholics. Know and follow your local governing ordinances. Legal incentives for responsible service have come in the form of state dram shop laws. Suppose that a bar patron, having drunk in excess, leaves a bar and attempts to drive home. If an accident occurs that results in injury or death to another person, financial liability falls not only on the intoxicated person, but also on the establishment in which the patron was served as well as on the server.

Responsible Policies

Service employees must be trained to spot intoxicated persons and refuse service. They must obey laws that prohibit serving beverage alcohol to minors and intoxicated individuals. Servers and bartenders should use good judgement in asking for proof of age and only accept authentic and common forms of identification such as a state I.D. card, a driver's license, or a military I.D. card.

Serving staff must follow their establishment's standardized beverage alcohol service policies to avoid serving a customer too much beverage alcohol. They should keep track of how much a customer drinks and observe any behavioral changes. People react differently to alcohol.

The way people react to alcohol depends on how much they consume as well as on the speed and the amount that enters the bloodstream. Alcohol can have an effect on the body in many ways. It can act as a depressant by reducing muscle or nerve activity. It can act as a diuretic, helping the body lose fluids and causing thirst. And it can cause vasolidation, a condition in which the small blood vessels on the surface of the skin dilate or swell, making the body lose heat. Signs that a person has consumed too much alcohol include:

- Significant changes in behavior.
- Relaxed inhibitions.
- Impaired judgement.
- Slowed reaction time.
- Impaired motor coordination.

Observation and good customer service are the keys to evaluating how alcohol is affecting a customer. When necessary, beverage servers should slow or stop beverage alcohol service to customers who demonstrate signs of intoxication. Never allow an intoxicated customer to drive away from your establishment.

As a manager, establish policies for serving beverage alcohol responsibly and train your staff thoroughly. Conduct meetings with employees on a regular basis to monitor the effectiveness of the alcohol service policies and modify them as needed. Standardizing beverage recipes, glassware, service procedures, and implementing last call policies establish a strong foundation for responsible beverage alcohol service and consistent profit.

Communication is the key to ensuring that your policies are carefully followed. Servers and bartenders should inform managers and co-workers on the next shift, or in other areas if an intoxicated customer has moved, if beverage alcohol service to a customer has been slowed or refused. They should inform customers about the key points of their policies, such as designated driver or alternate transportation policies. Good communication can help employees and managers avoid serving alcohol to minors and intoxicated individuals.

Responsible Promotions

Fear of third-party liability—and an increasing sense of responsibility by the food and beverage industry—has led many operations to promote safe drinking habits. Operators must use responsibility in advertising and coordinating product promotions. Use foresight—not hindsight—when planning promotions. Two-for-ones and pitchers of drinks increase risk. Some operators take advantage of the public's concern and offer promotions such as "Designated Driver" buttons, special nonalcoholic drink prices to drivers, and free taxi rides.

One promotional medium is the establishment of a designated driver program. A designated driver is a member of a group of bar patrons who chooses to abstain from drinking beverage alcohol. The designated driver assumes responsibility for seeing that others in the group arrive home safely. A designated driver program might include offering complimentary or discounted nonalcoholic drinks to the designated driver. Some operations provide their own designated driver, or a safe form of transportation such as a taxi or bus. Such promotions are likely to result in goodwill and frequent customers who know that the management is concerned about them.

Placing responsibility on patrons for their own drinking can also be part of responsible alcohol service. Sometimes people are not aware that they are drinking too much until it is too late. Helpful reminders, such as signs, breath-test devices, or table tents, can cause people to stop and think.

Incident Reports

When a beverage alcohol-related incident occurs, servers, bartenders, and managers may have to make decisions during difficult circumstances. Intervene as needed to discontinue beverage alcohol service and handle abusive and violent customers. Tactfully explain to a customer the need to cut off beverage alcohol service. Help ensure the customer's and others' safety by offering and arranging alternate transportation. Always call the police when violence occurs and when an intoxicated person drives away from the establishment. Finally, thoroughly document any beverage alcohol-related incident.

An incident report documents the facts of an incident and explains why certain actions were taken. Document any incident in which beverage alcohol service is refused or when alternate transportation is arranged. Also document when a minor presents false identification and when police are called to visit your establishment. Finally, always document the circumstances in which a customer suffers a beverage alcohol-related accident or becomes ill.

Write the report immediately after an incident occurs, while events and persons are clear in your mind. Detail as much information as possible about the incident. Explain in detail the customer's behavior and why beverage alcohol service was refused. Note the type of transportation arranged and why alternate transportation was chosen. Note that the customer took all of his or her belongings. Always include basic information such as the date, time, server on duty, server's station, names of customers and employees who witnessed the incident, and physical descriptions of all intoxicated customers involved.

If police were notified to handle the situation, record who spoke with the police officer, what information was provided, and the next step in the investigation process. If the customer suffered an accident or became ill and medical service was necessary, record the nature of the accident or illness and the customer's symptoms. Include the aid you provided, what medical service you called, when you made the call, when the service arrived, and what treatment they provided.

Whatever responsible alcohol service policy an operation adopts, all managers must train their employees thoroughly and back up their responsible behavior. Meet regularly with servers to discuss the effectiveness of the policies and revise them as necessary.

References

1. *Legal Aspects of Hospitality Management, Second Edition* by John E.H. Sherry ©1994 The Educational Foundation of the National Restaurant Association

2. *Presenting Service: The Ultimate Guide for the Foodservice Professional* by Lendal H. Kotschevar, FMP and Valentino Luciani ©1996 The Educational Foundation of the National Restaurant Association

3. *Bar Code: Serving Alcohol Responsibly, Manager Resource Guide* ©1996 The Educational Foundation of the National Restaurant Association

---

Learning Objectives

You will be asked to:

☆ State the standard procedures for controlling production volume.

☆ Explain procedures to ensure consistent food quality.

☆ Describe the quality factors that need to be checked before serving a finished menu item to a customer.

☆ Increase or decrease the yield of a standardized recipe.

☆ Predict production needs, given recent sales figures.

☆ List elements that must be included in a standardized recipe.

Food Quality

Quality control is based upon establishing and adhering to standards. Food quality begins with the purchasing process and ends with the finished, prepared menu item that is served to a customer. To ensure a high quality of food, you must have consistent quality products and production processes. An effective quality-control program increases overall control of the product, but more importantly, customer satisfaction as well.

Controlling Production Quantities

The success of the menu depends very much on how well the production system of an operation interprets what the menu offers. Conversely, successful production depends on how completely and accurately the menu itself is prepared, just as it depends on the purchasing system to provide the right materials at the right time at the right cost.

The goal of a production control system is to produce the number of portions likely to be sold on a given day. In controlling production volume, three standard procedures—maintaining a sales history, forecasting portion sales, and determining production quantities—are essential.

A sales history is a written record of the number of portions sold each time a given item appeared on a menu. Forecasting is used to predict what is likely to occur in the future. Based on documented sales history and present circumstances, this educated guess determines your production needs. For example, Fridays in the summer recently have meant approximately 280 for lunch at an operation. Typically, 32 percent of lunch customers order the Caesar salad. This translates to:

$$280 \times 0.32 = 89.6 \text{ customers}$$

So, the production staff can reasonably expect and prepare for approximately 90 Caesar salads.

With sales volume accurately predicted, necessary adjustments in purchasing and production can be made, reducing waste, spoilage, and overproduction. Predicting the total anticipated volume, referring to the sales history, evaluating the effects of surrounding conditions, and guessing the total business volume are necessary steps for successful forecasting. Used properly and accurately, forecasting enables a manager to track the popularity of existing menu items and to predict items that might prove popular in the future. This knowledge is especially helpful when revising a menu.

Good forecasts, recipe preparation, and portioning information must be provided to the production employees so that the they know the quantities, methods, and time required to prepare items. A production sheet sets the production goals for the chef and staff. It lists each menu item as well as the quantity expected to sell and is prepared to reflect determined forecasts. According to individual needs, these sheets may vary in complexity from one establishment to another. It also facilitates the coordination of management, purchasing, service, and other departments of the operation, which is essential in establishing and meeting production goals.

Controlling Production Standards

To produce exactly the same item each time it is offered to a patron, use standardized recipes and establish necessary controls. A standardized recipe lists ingredients and quantities to be used, as well as clear, detailed procedures to be followed each time an item is prepared. To develop a standardized recipe, pretest it and precalculate its cost. Recipes must be complete, precise, and carefully followed. They must specify cooking times and temperatures, the amount of food produced, the portion size, other necessary procedural information, and may include substitutions or variations. This ensures that the quality of an item remains consistent.

To make a recipe standard, analyze it thoroughly. Observe standard food proportions. For instance, if a cake has a sugar-to-flour ratio of 1.25:1, then recipes that deviate too far from that proportion will not be very good. Once a recipe has become standard, it can be modified to produce more or

fewer portions. When increasing or decreasing a recipe, however, it is important that only the *proportion* of the ingredients change and not the ingredients themselves.

To convert a recipe to yield a smaller or larger amount, start by dividing the desired yield by the original yield to determine the *conversion factor*. Suppose you want to convert a recipe that yields 90 portions so that it yields 250.

$$250 \div 90 = 2.78$$

This conversion factor is multiplied by each ingredient's original amount. Some ingredient amounts might need to be altered a bit because straight conversion can affect the flavor of the final product.

Even once a recipe has become standardized, its flavor, texture, color, tenderness, appearance, form, and temperature should be re-evaluated each time it is made and improvements should be made accordingly. A standardized recipe may also change if new products appear on the market. Continuous improvement of a recipe increases the food standard at any establishment.

Computers are valuable in the production process. Lists of standard portion sizes can be stored in a word processing file, printed when necessary, and distributed to production personnel. Standardized recipes can be stored, updated, or deleted as new recipes are developed. Spreadsheets are used to develop production forecasts. Additional uses for computers can be devised to suit the needs of individual establishments.

Timing is of the essence in the production process. Foods should be prepared at the proper time. Some can be prepared ahead and are often better if they are. Others should be prepared as close to service as possible. Foods that sit too long after preparation can lose culinary and nutritional quality and may become contaminated and unsafe. Production schedules will help indicate the amount of food required and the times it should be ready for service. Checks should be made to see how much is carried over after the service period. Runout times should be noted.

Monitoring production and taking corrective action is the responsibility of management. One method of ascertaining whether production standards are being followed is the use of a void sheet. Used to keep records of portions rejected by customers, the void sheet lists the server, the reason for the return, and the sales value of the affected menu item. Evaluating a void sheet can alert a manager to lapses in service and production as well as to items with poor customer appeal.

Finally, all finished products need to be checked for flavor, texture, color, tenderness, appearance, form, and temperature. The finished product should look, smell, and taste as you expected it to. Make sure all safety regulations have been adhered to throughout the production process.

References

1. *Management by Menu, Third Edition* by Lendal H. Kotschevar, FMP and Marcel R. Escoffier ©1994 The Educational Foundation of The National Restaurant Association

2. *Quantity Food Production, Planning, and Management, Second Edition* by John B. Knight and Lendal H. Kotschevar, FMP ©1989 Van Nostrand Reinhold

Learning Objectives

You will be asked to:

☆ Categorize foods according to their USDA grade.

☆ Recognize the reason for par stock inventory.

☆ Describe the information required on a purchase specification.

☆ Compare purchase specifications to product specifications.

☆ Select the most important factor in determining an amount to order.

☆ State an advantage of "sourcing."

☆ Discuss reasons for conducting vendor audits.

☆ Choose a correct receiving procedure.

☆ Compare several receiving policy alternatives and choose the most effective.

☆ Determine when a shipment of fish, meat, or produce is fresh and acceptable.

☆ Distinguish between a physical inventory system and a perpetual inventory system.

☆ Define the "first-in, first-out" rule.

☆ Explain how to effectively control inventory replacements of spirits.

☆ State the reason for completing a product requisition form.

Inventory Functions

Whether the manager performs or oversees these functions, a good understanding of standards and practices helps to ensure efficient overall kitchen management.

Purchasing Food and Beverages

Expert purchasing requires knowledge of the production, processing, and marketing of products, their use in the establishment, and menu pricing. The buyer needs to know about how the market operates, about markups, seasonal factors, and where to find specific items of the best quality for the best price. A good buyer is constantly in search of products that will simplify preparation and handling, improve quality, and facilitate services. A buyer should also be active in analyzing cost and performance factors and in sorting out procedures that will improve the purchasing function.

Selecting a Supplier

Smaller operations generally employ informal methods of food and beverage purchasing. This open-type buying is conducted through talks between the buyer and supplier. Knowing the market is very important to the informal buyer, who should compare prices, quality, and quantity before making any purchases. A larger operation most likely will depend on formal, or competitive buying, which involves a number of written agreements. A buyer also needs to consider the specific needs of the operations.

Sourcing, or one-stop shopping, means that the buyer will try to purchase as many items as possible from one supplier. The advantages of this purchasing procedure include reduction of ordering cost, less paperwork, the opportunity to place standing orders, less receiving activity, fewer deliveries, and less opportunity for error. However, one drawback is that the buyer is restricted to the supplier's selection of goods. Also, the buyer is not as motivated to shop around for the best prices or quality once a comfortable relationship has been established with the source supplier. So, the buyer could be spending more money over a long period of time.

In informal buying situations, periodic negotiations with a supplier about price, delivery schedules, or product quality will usually build mutual respect between you and also assure you the best value. An establishment's budget will often largely determine its negotiating power. Negotiations should by no means entail browbeating or hostile ultimatums; a diplomatic, cordial relationship with any supplier is the most effective tool for receiving the best value. While negotiating takes time and effort, the benefits can be considerable.

Above all, a manager needs to be aware of the many aspects affecting the purchasing process and decide which procedure is the best for his operation. No one can dictate the criteria a buyer uses when selecting suppliers.

Purchase Specifications

Buyers indicate the quality and price of the foods they wish to purchase on purchase specifications. These should include the name of the product, size, packaging, and quality or grade desired. The specification must be as detailed as possible so that the buyer receives the most appropriate quality of product. Usually, a specification should include:

☐ Name of the item.

☐ Quantity needed.

☐ Grade of the item, brand, or other quality information.

☐ Packaging method, size package, and special requirements.

☐ Basis for price—by the pound, case, piece, dozen, etc.

Miscellaneous factors required to receive the correct item, such as the number of days beef should be aged, the region in which the item is produced, or the requirement that all items be inspected for wholesomeness.

Buying quality can be defined in different ways, such as by brand name or by grade. Federal standards are usually the basis for grading systems. *Standard of identity* is also an important method for determining quality. Standard of identity is a legal description of what an item is. For example, no manufacturer of egg noodles can use the term "egg" to describe noodles unless the noodles contain five and one-half percent dry egg solids.

Because meat is likely to be the most expensive inventory item in an operation, receiving exactly what you want is crucial. The U.S. Department of Agriculture (USDA) grades meat according to its wholesomeness and quality. *(See Exhibit 1.1.)*

The grades of beef, veal, and lamb most often used in food service are Prime, Choice, and Select. These are the highest-quality and highest-priced cuts.

Fresh fish has shiny skin; firm, elastic flesh; bright, clear, protruding eyes; bright, red, clear gills; and a mild, non-fishy odor. Fresh fish is delivered on crushed, self-draining ice, and is stored on fresh ice. It is important that fish is properly stored to avoid spoilage. Most shellfish are purchased live, and must be checked to make sure they are fresh when received. Tightly closed shells indicate freshness; any delivery containing many open shells should be rejected. To help ensure safety of shellfish and crustaceans, the Food and Drug Administration (FDA) requires that all establishments retain dated shell stock tags for ninety days after use of the shellfish.

Because fruits and vegetables are highly perishable, purchasing procedures and schedules must become second nature to the manager. Quality indicators for fruits and vegetables vary from one item to another, but there are some common traits. Fruits and vegetables should be free of bruises, mold, brown or soft spots, and pest damage (unless they are grown organically, without herbicides and pesticides). The color and texture should be appropriate to the particular type of fruit or vegetable. Any attached leaves should be firm and not wilted. Fruits should be plump, not shriveled.

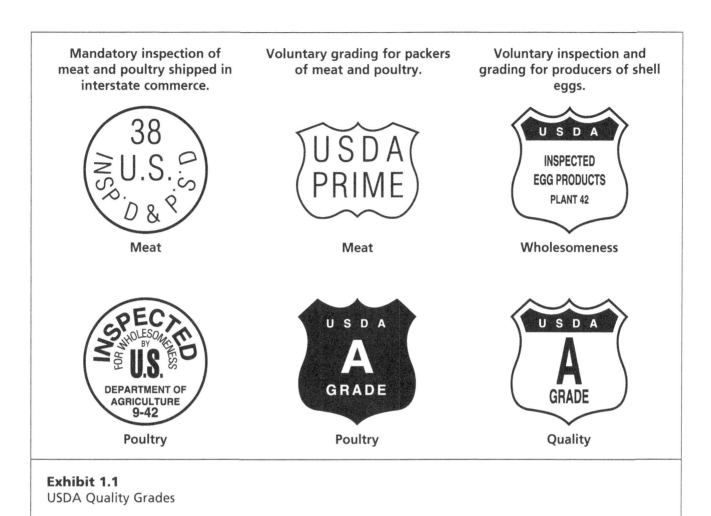

Mandatory inspection of meat and poultry shipped in interstate commerce.	Voluntary grading for packers of meat and poultry.	Voluntary inspection and grading for producers of shell eggs.
Meat	Meat	Wholesomeness
Poultry	Poultry	Quality

Exhibit 1.1
USDA Quality Grades

Extra care must be taken when purchasing, receiving, and storing fresh shell eggs. The quality grades given to eggs are governed by strict regulations, and all foodservice professionals should be familiar with these grades and regulations. Shell eggs must be clean and should have no noticeable odor. Whole shell eggs must be delivered under refrigeration and placed in refrigerated storage immediately upon receipt. (For detailed information concerning the receiving and handling of eggs, refer to the FDA's Model Food Code for shell eggs and your local code.)

Specifications are not normally used to purchase liquor and other beverages because these are most often bought by brand name. Purchasers of liquor and other beverages should have a thorough understanding of everything served by their operation—whiskey, vodka, gin, and other spirits; wines and their derivatives, such as wine coolers; beer; and nonalcoholic beverages.

All operators submit their written request for items on a purchase order. This should be used to verify all deliveries.

Receiving Food and Beverages

The primary purpose of receiving is to verify that the quantity, quality, and price of items are consistent with the orders placed. In many operations, a receiving clerk is employed to perform this verification. It is important that one person be trained thoroughly and held responsible for receiving deliveries.

As specified by the operation's policies, the manager or employee delegated to receive deliveries should:

- Compare the vendor's invoice to the delivery.

- Compare the invoice to the purchase order to ensure the correct quality and quantity has been delivered.

- Log all items delivered on the receiving report.

- See that all items are delivered to the correct department for immediate use, or stored properly.

The receiving clerk needs to compare all deliveries to the vendor's invoice, or bill, which should list prices to be checked upon receipt of goods. Items should be weighed or counted to determine quantity and carefully checked to determine whether their quality matches that which has been outlined in the standard purchase specifications. Unit prices on the invoice are then compared to those quoted on the purchase orders. Once the receiving clerk has verified the quantity, quality, and price of each item, he stamps the invoice to acknowledge this verification.

The receiving clerk's report is an important accounting document that summarizes all that is received during a given period. Depending on the delivery schedules of the establishment, this report may be completed daily or weekly. Receiving personnel require ongoing training to maintain standards. Monitoring is required to check and correct the performance of daily routines.

When produce arrives, it is important to check that all deliveries are fresh and of high quality. Most establishments employ special controls for receiving meats, poultry, fish, and shellfish, which are usually the most costly group of foods. Often, the receiving clerk tags each item before it is stored, thus providing tighter control.

Because liquor and beverages are particularly attractive targets of pilferage and theft, they should be received by responsible, accountable employees and taken immediately to a secure storage facility.

Once a delivery has been inspected and stored, there should be controls established to audit a vendor's invoice. Just as the quality of the delivery was checked against the purchase specifications, the prices on the invoice must be checked against the quoted prices. Also, the payment terms and any promised discounts need to be verified.

Maintaining Inventory

To maintain quality control over storing, standards must be established. The maintenance of proper internal conditions includes temperature, storage containers, shelving, and cleanliness.

All inventories must be maintained and controlled regularly. A *physical inventory* requires managers or employees to count all of the items in storage by hand, usually monthly. A *perpetual inventory* is maintained through stock record cards that document all deliveries and issues by date. Bin cards, often used in liquor storage areas, are similar to stock record cards, and record the name and type of the item, delivery dates, and issues. In addition to these inventory control measures, many operations maintain a par stock of particular items. The par stock is the quantity needed on hand to ensure an adequate supply between delivery dates. The par stock amount is generally dictated by suppliers' delivery schedules and forecasted sales volume.

Issuing Food and Beverages from Inventory

All inventory items should be moved out of storage through a systematic issuing process. Stocks must be properly dated and rotated. The system of first in, first out FIFO ensures that older items are used before new items. Placing new items behind older ones facilitates this process.

Product requisition forms often are filled out by kitchen personnel, indicating exactly what items are needed for production, and given to the manager or another appointed employee. This practice prevents the unauthorized pilfering of inventory items, and allows management to keep track of what is being used and when items must be reordered. To keep track of liquor issues, some operators require employees to return empty bottles with their replacement requisitions.

Some operations have replaced product requisition forms with computerized systems that include labeling and tracking items by its universal product code (UPC) label, or bar code. Some systems even have the capacity to order par stock and other items as necessary directly from a personal computer. Spreadsheet software packages can be helpful in maintaining a perpetual inventory system. The applications of computers in the foodservice industry continue to expand and diversify.

References

1. *Purchasing: Selection and Procurement for the Hospitality Industry, Fourth Edition* by John Stefanelli ©1997 John Wiley and Sons, Inc.

2. *Quantity Food Production, Planning, and Management, Second Edition* by John B. Knight and Lendal H. Kotschevar, FMP ©1989 Van Nostrand Reinhold

3. *Principles of Food, Beverage, and Labor Cost Controls, Sixth Edition* by Paul R. Dittmer and Gerald G. Griffin, FMP ©1999 John Wiley and Sons, Inc.

4. *Management by Menu, Third Edition* by Lendal H. Kotschevar, FMP and Marcel R. Escoffier ©1994 The Educational Foundation of the National Restaurant Association

Facility Maintenance

Responsible planning and intelligently designed facilities help create a positive work and service environment. Similarly, thoughtful purchase, proper maintenance, and timely replacement of equipment will affect the efficiency and effectiveness of a foodservice operation.

Attention to cleaning and maintenance procedures should be part of every operation's daily routine. This is made easier when building and equipment finishes are durable, easily cleaned, resistant to damage by abrasive cleaners, and resistant to grease buildup. Employees should be able to comfortably see and reach all parts of equipment and facilities comfortably.

Maintaining Facilities

The facility should have a master cleaning schedule that details what will be cleaned, when, how, and by whom. The schedule should include floors, walls, ceilings, work surfaces, hoods and filters, grease traps, restroom fixtures, windowsflevery part of the facility. A facility and equipment inspection checklist provides for continual and systematic checking of the entire operation for safety, cleanliness, and maintenance problems.

Selecting Equipment

The investment you make in equipment is crucial to the success of your operation. You must know what is available and what will best fit your needs. *(See Exhibit 1.2.)*

Reasons for selecting a new piece of equipment include:

☐ Outfitting a new facility.

☐ Replacing worn or inefficient equipment.

☐ Responding to changes in the menu or volume of business.

☐ Reducing costs (labor, maintenance, and energy).

Function	Major Pieces of Equipment
Receiving and storage	Scales, conveyers, hand trucks, ramps, forklift truck, cart, shelving, walk-in and reach-in refrigerator and freezer
Prepreparation and preparation	Mixer, oven, chopper, tilting frying pan, steam-jacketed kettle, scale, slicers, peelers, meat saw
Final preparation	Steamer (no-/low-/high-pressure), bain-marie, broiler, grill, microwave oven, fryer, range, conventional oven, convection oven
Service area/cafeteria	Coffee urn, hot food table, ice machine, roll warmer, beverage dispensers
Warewashing	Dishwashing and warewashing machine, pot sink
Waste removal	Garbage disposal, pulper, trash compactor

Exhibit 1.2
Overview of Major Equipment Needs

A careful evaluation of available alternatives is important in order to select the correct piece of equipment at the lowest possible cost. If the yearly cost of the equipment will be returned to the food operation through increased productivity and a better quality food product, then the equipment cost is justifiable.

NSF International (formerly the National Sanitation Foundation) provides its seal of approval to manufactured equipment meeting its criteria for sanitary and safe construction. The seal is not mandatory for foodservice equipment, but NSF International approval is a recognized standard of quality in the industry. Underwriters Laboratories (UL) also provides sanitation classification listings for equipment found in compliance with NSF International standards. Managers should look for the NSF International mark or the UL Sanitation Classification mark on commercial foodservice equipment. *(See Exhibit 1.3.)*

It is the responsibility of the manager to know the general features on which NSF International bases its standards. These include:

Exhibit 1.3
NSF and UL Logos.

☐ Equipment must be easy to clean.

☐ All food-contact surfaces must be smooth, nontoxic, nonabsorbent, corrosion resistant, and stable and must not cause changes in color, odor, or taste of the food.

☐ Internal corners and edges exposed to food must be rounded off.

- All food-contact surfaces must be smooth and free of pits, crevices, ledges, inside threads and shoulders, bolts, and rivet heads.

- Coating materials must be nontoxic and cleanable and must resist cracking and chipping.

- Equipment must be easy to disassemble to encourage frequent, thorough cleaning.

Well-written equipment specifications can help you obtain a piece of equipment that will do the job you want in the most economical way possible, with an investment that is not unnecessarily high. The specification document should include a complete, detailed description of the equipment needed; and the conditions of the purchase. The conditions of the purchase include quality assurance, details of inspection, performance testing, how the installation will be accomplished and by whom, warranties, and all other terms of the agreement. Files should be kept for all written records.

Maintaining Equipment

Over the useful life of a piece of equipment, its operating costs usually will be double the purchase price or more. How long a piece of equipment will last depends mostly on the use and maintenance of the equipment. With a solid maintenance program, equipment can last longer and operate with greater energy efficiency, lower cost, and higher sanitation levels.

Maintaining equipment easily and effectively depends on:

- Choice of original fabrication methods and materials: Nonporous surfaces, few seams, etc.

- Design: Few crevices that collect soil and food, streamlined utility connections, easy access to all parts.

- Procedures: A clean-as-you-work policy to reduce buildup. Most manufacturers' representatives will demonstrate operation and cleaning methods when equipment is installed.

To develop a maintenance plan, consult manufacturers' manuals to determine, for example, how often to oil parts or change filters. Set up a schedule for performing these tasks, for cleaning, and for inspection. Make repairs promptly and adjust as necessary for efficient operation. In some circumstances it may be more expedient and economical to engage a good service provider specializing in the maintenance and repair of certain pieces of equipment.

References

1. *Design and Layout of Foodservice Facilities* by John C. Birchfield ©1988 John Wiley and Sons, Inc.

2. *Quantity Food Production, Planning, and Management, Second Edition* by John B. Knight and Lendal H. Kotschevar, FMP ©1989 Van Nostrand Reinhold

Review Questions

The following questions are structured to draw from your experience and education as much as this manual's content. Some questions may also prompt review of a topic listed in the references at the end of each section.

Customer Service

1. Which of the following is the most crucial aspect of any server's job?

    A. Remembering specific orders

    B. Meeting people's needs

    C. Learning correct techniques

    D. Reporting tips correctly

2. When people choose among competing food services when they want to eat out, they tend to make their decisions based on differences in

    A. quality of food.

    B. mood or décor.

    C. quality of service.

    D. location.

3. Companies generally define their business goals and target market in a(n)

    A. organization chart.

    B. balance sheet.

    C. income statement.

    D. mission statement.

4. Of the following, it is most important for an organization's mission statement to be communicated to

    A. upper-level managers.

    B. employees at all levels.

    C. supervisors and unit managers.

    D. external public.

5. Which of the following is the best example of a server anticipating a guest's need?

    A. A server brings water to a table at which three people have just been seated.

    B. A server describes in detail the ingredients in all of the evening's specials.

    C. A server answers a guest's questions about areas of interest and entertainment in the restaurant's community.

    D. A server recommends quickly prepared menu items after a guest says she is on the way to a sporting event.

6. Servers should take their cue in helping guests with disabilities from

    A. more experienced servers.

    B. the guest with the disability.

    C. management.

    D. the operation's policies.

7. Servers should have thorough product knowledge so that they are able to

    A. fill in for kitchen workers when necessary.

    B. train in other areas of the operation.

    C. explain the menu to guests and answer their questions.

    D. handle sensitive guest situations tactfully.

8. The most efficient way to record guest reservations is to
   A. record the party's name, number of guests, time of arrival, and special needs.
   B. record the party's name and tell the caller when you will seat them.
   C. use the answering machine to handle reservations.
   D. allow guests to make reservations up to one year in advance.

9. When customers arrive at your full-service restaurant ten minutes before closing, employees should
   A. inform them that you are about to close.
   B. seat them near the door and tell them they can only order quickly cooked menu items.
   C. turn up the lights and turn off background music so they know you are about to close.
   D. serve them as you would all customers.

10. Which of the following is the most likely sign that a guest is unhappy or dissatisfied with service?
   A. Sitting with crossed arms
   B. Chatting with guests
   C. Using the server's name
   D. Lingering over coffee

11. If customers have been asking for new pieces of silverware because theirs are dirty, the manager should
   A. inspect the replacement silverware and polish it with a clean towel.
   B. explain to the customer that all the silverware has been sanitized, though some pieces may look dirty.
   C. see to it that the offending silverware is thrown away.
   D. check the silverware-washing procedure to ensure that everything is working properly.

12. When a customer complains, the first thing an employee or manager should do is
   A. listen to everything the customer says.
   B. let the customer know who is at fault.
   C. tell the customer the operation's point of view.
   D. stick to the operation's rules and policies.

13. A customer has complained to you about something that you know was the fault of an employee. You should
   A. apologize immediately.
   B. tell the customer whose fault it was.
   C. criticize the employee.
   D. deny the problem.

14. When receiving complaints from angry customers, it is best to
   A. listen fully to their description of the problem.
   B. try to keep them from venting emotions.
   C. point out that it is not necessary to behave angrily.
   D. defend the operation's policies.

Menu Planning and Management

15. All customer complaints must be
   A. handled by the manager on duty.
   B. resolved promptly.
   C. resolved by the employee who is first contacted.
   D. responded to in writing.

16. The major feature of the California menu is that
    A. all items are available at all hours.
    B. it is used on weekends and holidays.
    C. certain items are available only during peak hours of operation.
    D. all items are native Californian recipes.

17. Which of the following operations is most likely to use a limited menu?
    A. Fine-dining restaurant
    B. Quick-service operation
    C. Hospital cafeteria
    D. Elementary or secondary school

18. A menu item's cost divided by its revenue gives the item's
    A. demand.
    B. gross profit.
    C. food cost percentage.
    D. selling price.

19. Which of the following is the most customary selling price to include on a full-service menu?
    A. $6.00
    B. $6.25
    C. $6.80
    D. $6.95

20. It is important that an operation's menu reflect which of the following?
    A. Operating costs
    B. Theme and atmosphere of the operation
    C. Number of servers on duty during each shifts
    D. Competitors' business philosophies and how they differ

21. Which of the following is considered a disadvantage of script and italic typeface?
    A. It conveys too casual a tone and atmosphere.
    B. It is more expensive to print than plain type.
    C. It is more difficult to read than plain type.
    D. It tends not to emphasize content to readers.

22. Standard portion sizes ensure that the customer receives consistent
    A. flavor.
    B. quantity.
    C. price.
    D. texture.

23. If a menu item's food cost is $0.80 and the desired food cost percentage is 28 percent, what is its menu price (rounded to the nearest $0.10)?
    A. $3.00
    B. $2.90
    C. $2.80
    D. $2.70

24. A food service's menu item has a food cost of $4.34, and the operation's desired food cost percentage is 34 percent. Based on this, what should the item's selling price be?
    A. $10.95
    B. $11.95
    C. $12.95
    D. $13.95

25. An operator marks up its wines by 60 percent. If a certain wine costs the operation $17.00, what will its selling price be (rounded to the nearest dollar)?
    A. $23
    B. $25
    C. $27
    D. $29

26. A yield analysis is used primarily to determine
    A. the price of a menu item.
    B. the tasks involved in preparing a menu item.
    C. how much usable food is contained in a purchased quantity.
    D. the raw cost of a menu item.

27. What is the portion cost of a 10-ounce serving obtained from a 4-pound cut of veal costing $15.69?
    A. $2.15
    B. $2.45
    C. $2.75
    D. $2.95

28. One Reuben sandwich calls for 6 ounces of sliced corned beef. How many pounds of sliced corned beef are needed to prepare 140 sandwiches?
    A. 22 lbs.
    B. 37.5 lbs.
    C. 41 lbs.
    D. 52.5 lbs.

29. Which of the following menu items should a server recommend to a guest on a high-fiber, low-fat diet?
    A. Couscous with Steamed Broccoli, Snow Peas, and Mushrooms
    B. Linguine with Tomato Cream Sauce
    C. Lasagna with Beef and Italian Sausage
    D. Pizza with Canadian Bacon, Pineapple, and Mozzarella Cheese

30. All of the following statements are true *except*
    A. keeping track of menu items sold is important in analyzing sales to cost ratios.
    B. once a menu is developed and printed, the items available on it should never change.
    C. pricing methods should consider costs.
    D. storage space must be taken into consideration when developing a menu.

Responsible Alcohol Service

31. Employees who work in establishments that serve beverage alcohol should know
    A. their state's laws about serving minors or intoxicated guests.
    B. that the sale of beverage alcohol to minors is legal in many states.
    C. that parents are always allowed to serve their children beverage alcohol in restaurants.
    D. that in many states, it is legal to serve an adult to and past the point of intoxication.

32. An establishment can be held liable under third-party liability when
    A. an intoxicated guest is injured by an employee of the establishment.
    B. an intoxicated guest injures himself or herself after leaving the establishment.
    C. someone is injured by a non-intoxicated guest after the guest leaves the establishment.
    D. someone is injured by an intoxicated guest who became intoxicated in the establishment.

33. Courts tend to hold establishments liable for

    A. charging too much for beverage alcohol.

    B. refusing to serve beverage alcohol to an intoxicated guest.

    C. observing guests' behaviors.

    D. not serving beverage alcohol to a suspected minor.

34. Why is it important for servers to talk to their guests whenever they bring them beverage alcohol?

    A. Guests are more likely to become angry with friendly servers who stop beverage alcohol service.

    B. Guests may drink more slowly and enjoy the taste.

    C. Servers can more easily tell if a guest's behavior is changing.

    D. Guests are more likely to order beverage alcohol.

35. Counting drinks is not an effective way of controlling service to a guest if the bartender

    A. uses different sized glasses for different drinks.

    B. free pours.

    C. uses automatic pouring devices.

    D. uses measuring jiggers.

36. To serve beverage alcohol consistently, you should

    A. standardize drink recipes.

    B. serve all drinks in the same type of glassware.

    C. free pour to save time.

    D. always announce last call when there are five or fewer guests left in the establishment.

37. Which of the following guests should have beverage alcohol service stopped?

    A. Ted consumes two beverage alcohol drinks and orders two more.

    B. Melba suddenly stops giggling.

    C. Walter wants to buy a round of drinks for two Cubs fans at another table.

    D. Susan is telling jokes a little too loudly.

38. When should door staff ask a guest to sign his or her name to check it against the signature on the I.D.?

    A. When the guest looks too young to purchase beverage alcohol.

    B. When the guest has been drinking before coming to the establishment.

    C. When the guest hesitates or is uncertain in answering questions about information on the I.D.

    D. When the I.D. is not a picture I.D.

39. What is the final step after a difficult situation involving alcohol has been resolved?

    A. Call the police.

    B. Clean up any mess.

    C. Arrange for alternate transportation.

    D. Fill out an incident report form.

40. When should you write an incident report?

    A. One day after the incident occurred.

    B. Immediately after the incident is resolved.

    C. When a criminal charge or lawsuit is filed.

    D. At the end of your shift.

Food Quality

41. Sales forecasts are most commonly based on which of the following?

    A. Sales histories

    B. Desired profits

    C. Industry reports

    D. Industry averages

42. Managers use production forecasts to ensure that

    A. standard production procedures are followed.

    B. appropriate quantities of food are prepared.

    C. the sales history in accurate.

    D. enough employees are scheduled.

43. Records of the number of customers served and number of portions sold of each menu item during past periods are called

    A. production sheets.

    B. business plans.

    C. feasibility studies.

    D. sales histories.

44. Standardized bowls, cups, and ladles are examples of which of the following standards?

    A. Quality

    B. Productivity

    C. Quantity

    D. Production

45. Which of the following formulas determines the portion cost of a recipe?

    A. Cost of ingredients ÷ Number of portions

    B. Number of portions ÷ Cost of ingredients

    C. Hidden costs ÷ Cost of ingredients

    D. Hidden costs ÷ Number of portions

46. A recipe for cream of cauliflower soup costs a total of $16.78. If the recipe yields 24 portions, what is the recipe's portion cost?

    A. $0.66

    B. $0.68

    C. $0.70

    D. $0.72

47. At the bar, portion control should always include

    A. specified recipes.

    B. an automatic dispenser system.

    C. a bartender's own measurements.

    D. using house brands instead of call brands.

48. A recipe for 6 stuffed pork chops includes 4 oz. Dijon mustard. If the recipe is converted to yield 9 pork chops, how much mustard will be called for?

    A. 4.5 oz.

    B. 6 oz.

    C. 8 oz.

    D. 12 oz.

49. If 7.2 ounces of sole are used to make one stuffed sole dinner, how many pounds of sole are needed to make enough portions to fill a weekly forecast of 500?

    A. 69.5 lbs.

    B. 225 lbs.

    C. 270 lbs.

    D. 360 lbs.

50. The most important reason for weighing raw hamburger patties as they are made is to

    A. control portion size.

    B. calculate shrinkage rates.

    C. back up menu claims about weight.

    D. determine the precise cooking time needed.

51. A restaurant serves an average of 320 meals during each dinner period. Menu analysis shows that 20 percent of all guests order the chicken enchilada dinner. How many chicken enchilada dinners should be prepared for an average day?

    A. 56
    B. 64
    C. 70
    D. 82

52. Pieces of minced vegetable are

    A. very thin slices.
    B. about 1″×1″×2″.
    C. very small and fairly uniform in size.
    D. not all the same size and shape.

53. If held too long on the steam table, cornstarch-thickened sauces are likely to

    A. become too thick.
    B. become too thin.
    C. develop a starchy taste.
    D. darken unattractively.

54. Which of the following combinations contains the best balance of flavor, texture, and appearance?

    A. Duchesse potatoes and pureed squash
    B. Cream of celery soup and broiled chicken breast
    C. Cucumbers in yogurt-garlic dressing and garlic bread
    D. Stuffed tomato appetizer and meatballs in herbed tomato sauce

Inventory Functions

55. Multi-unit chains generally are organized for purchasing differently from independent operations in that they

    A. assign several different managers per unit to perform purchasing functions.
    B. have an extra level of management above the purchaser.
    C. tend to have simpler and more streamlined purchasing processes.
    D. have need of higher-quality products.

56. The act of "sourcing," or establishing a relationship between a buyer and a supplier, generally is

    A. beneficial to both the buyer and the seller.
    B. considered unethical.
    C. engaged in almost all countries except the United States.
    D. sought by buyers but not suppliers.

57. When calculating the amount to order, managers must consider

    A. the amount required for the upcoming period.
    B. how much work the steward can handle.
    C. how much business they want to give a particular supplier.
    D. the amount they used in the previous period.

58. A par stock of some inventory items is maintained in order to

    A. keep money in stock and not in cash.
    B. ensure an adequate supply between delivery dates.
    C. take advantage of good prices.
    D. balance the amount of items charged to directs.

59. USDA grading of meat products provides information concerning the meat's

    A. freshness.

    B. quality.

    C. cholesterol content.

    D. area of origin.

60. Specifications indicate which of the following?

    A. Where purchased items are to be delivered

    B. Par stock levels and when regular orders are to be delivered

    C. Which of an operation's employees are authorized to accept deliveries

    D. Name, amount, brand, packaging, grade, and other characteristics of items to be purchased

61. All deliveries should be checked against the vendor's invoice and the

    A. purchase order.

    B. product requisition form.

    C. production sheet.

    D. inventory list.

62. A copy of the standard purchase specifications is a necessary tool of the receiving clerk so that the

    A. quantity of food items can be checked.

    B. price of food items can be checked.

    C. quality of food items can be checked.

    D. invoice can be verified.

63. Which of the following generally is the most effective receiving policy to follow?

    A. Staggering delivery hours and days so that receiving personnel are not overwhelmed or rushed

    B. Scheduling delivery hours and days on weekends so that supplies are in place for the business week ahead

    C. Not locking delivery hours and times into prearranged schedules so that both buyers and suppliers can be flexible

    D. Keeping the accountant or bookkeeper separated from the receiving process to help control security

64. Which of the following is a sign that a shipment of fish is fresh and acceptable to receive?

    A. Soft flesh

    B. Fishy scent

    C. Gray gills

    D. Clear, bright eyes

65. Placing bar codes on inventory items helps to

    A. keep items secure from internal pilferage.

    B. control movement of items in and out of storage.

    C. keep items secure from outside theft.

    D. control storage temperatures and humidity.

66. The "first in, first out" rule refers to

    A. purchasing items from only one supplier.

    B. using food supplies in the order they are received.

    C. promoting employees by seniority.

    D. storing potentially hazardous foods below 40°F (4°C).

67. Kitchen employees let a purchaser know what supplies are needed by listing them on a(n)

    A. product requisition form.

    B. purchase specification.

    C. bin card.

    D. invoice.

68. When you are issuing spirits, the most effective way to ensure that items requested are replacing items used is to

    A. require employees to return empty bottles with requisitions.

    B. analyze the beverage mix on a point-of-sale system.

    C. maintain a perpetual inventory of all beverages.

    D. maintain a par stock of all beverages.

69. You have ordered some frozen tuna steaks for your restaurant. When the delivery arrives, you notice that there is excessive frost and ice in the package. You refuse the delivery. Why?

    A. You suspect that the steaks may have been contaminated with a cleaning compound.

    B. You suspect the fish may contain toxic levels of iron.

    C. You suspect that the steaks have not been held at the appropriate temperature and may cause foodborne illness if you serve them.

    D. You believe the supply company may have treated the steaks with an unauthorized preservative.

Facility Maintenance

70. The most important factor in locating a kitchen is placing it

    A. adjacent to the receiving area.

    B. central to all other areas.

    C. distant from street or parking lot entries.

    D. near cleanup facilities.

71. In production area layouts, it is most important to shorten the distance between final preparation and the

    A. warewashing area.

    B. pre-preparation area.

    C. service area.

    D. salad-preparation area.

72. Which factor usually is most influential in the type of cooking equipment chosen by a food service?

    A. Number of employees

    B. Local ordinances

    C. Utility rates

    D. The menu

73. Equipment specifications should include a complete description of the equipment needed and

    A. price.

    B. conditions of the purchase.

    C. color of the item.

    D. where the equipment should be shipped.

74. The most important consideration in writing equipment specifications is

    A. writing clearly and exactly what is needed.

    B. making them as brief as possible.

    C. making them general enough to be flexible.

    D. arranging the categories.

75. Large equipment mounted on small legs is inefficient because

    A. more energy is used.

    B. it is difficult to clean under.

    C. it is expensive.

    D. only electricity can be used.

76. Generally, the most cost-effective way to maintain equipment is to

    A. implement a program of preventative maintenance.

    B. replace equipment when it breaks down.

    C. employ a full-time equipment troubleshooter.

    D. maintain all the equipment yourself.

77. A preventative equipment maintenance program is important primarily because it

    A. eliminates the need to replace equipment.

    B. is required by local health departments.

    C. reduces the frequency of equipment replacement.

    D. provides opportunities for employee training.

78. Of the following, the manager's first resource for repairing and maintaining a piece of equipment is

    A. a local service company.

    B. a restaurant equipment vendor.

    C. a colleague who uses the same equipment.

    D. the original equipment manual.

79. A manager prepares a checklist for cleaning equipment that includes dates for cleaning and maintenance, and signature lines for the task performer. What is missing?

    A. A directive that only the manager should clean equipment

    B. Specifications for replacing equipment

    C. The price of each piece of equipment

    D. A description of how to clean and service the equipment

Answer Key

Customer Service

1. B
2. C
3. D
4. B
5. A
6. B
7. C
8. A
9. D
10. A
11. D
12. A
13. A
14. A

Menu Planning and Management

15. B
16. A
17. B
18. C
19. D
20. B
21. C
22. B
23. B
24. C
25. C
26. C
27. B
28. D
29. A
30. B

Responsible Alcohol Service

31. A
32. D
33. C
34. C
35. B
36. A
37. A
38. C
39. D
40. B

Food Quality

41. A
42. B
43. D
44. C
45. A
46. C
47. A
48. B
49. B
50. A
51. B
52. C
53. B
54. B

Inventory Functions

55. B
56. A
57. A
58. B
59. B
60. D
61. A
62. C
63. A
64. D
65. B
66. B
67. A
68. A
69. C

Facility Maintainance

70. B
71. C
72. D
73. B
74. A
75. B
76. A
77. C
78. D
79. D

Chapter 2 Outline

I. **Food Safety**

    A   Food Safety and the Law

    B.   Contamination and Spoilage

        1.   Foodborne Illness

        2.   Potentially Hazardous Foods

    C.   Keeping Food Safe from Storage to Service

        1.   Temperature Abuse

        2.   Storing Food Safely

            a.   Refrigerated Storage

            b.   Freezer and Dry Storage

        3.   Handling Food Safely

        4.   Principles of Safe Cooking

        5.   Cooling and Reheating Methods

        6.   Holding Foods

        7.   HACCP

    D.   Sanitation

        1.   Clean vs. Sanitary

        2.   Training Employees

        3.   Good Personal Hygiene

        4.   Reporting Employee Illnesses

    E.   Responding to an Outbreak of Foodborne Illness

    F.   Waste Management

II. **Safety and Security**

    A.   Public and Employee Liability

    B.   The Hazard Communication Standard (HCS)

    C.   A Safety Program

        1.   Developing a Safety Program

        2.   Documenting and Monitoring a Safety Program

        3.   Safety Training

        4.   Emergency Training and Procedures

    D.   Security

        1.   Facility Security

        2.   Preventing Theft

III. **Review Questions**

Chapter 2
Risk Management

Learning Objectives

You will be asked to:

☆ Demonstrate the correct managerial action during an official inspection.

☆ Give examples of who or what prohibits unsafe food handling procedures.

☆ Outline key elements of a reasonable care defense.

Food Safety

Food Safety and the Law

Two powerful motives for protecting customers, foodhandlers, and foodservice establishments are laws and the financial burden placed on operators for public safety. State laws, county and municipal health codes, and municipal ordinances with a provision for fines or closure for violations prohibit unsafe food handling practices for food services. These laws are intended to protect both the public and operators.

The Food and Drug Administration (FDA) writes the *Model Food Code,* which provides recommendations for foodservice regulations throughout the United States. However, in the United States, most food regulations that affect foodservice operations are written at the state level. Each individual state decides whether to adopt the Model Food Code or some modified form of it. Finally, the state regulations are then enforced by a local agency responsible for enforcing health codes—usually a city, county, or state health department. Managers must contact local health departments to find out which specific regulations apply to their operations.

The state or local health department can conduct operational inspections at any time during the year. The health inspector is trained in sanitation principles, scientific methods, and public health, and represents the department. In most cases, the inspector arrives without prior warning. Always ask for identification and inquire about the purpose of the visit; it is important to know whether the inspection is routine, is a result of a customer complaint, or is due to some other reason. Accompany the inspector during the inspection, take notes, and cooperate with his or her requests. Keep the relationship professional.

Be ready to provide records should the inspector request them. Discuss violations and time frames for correction with the inspector. Make it clear that you are willing to correct problems. Finally, follow up. Determine why each violation occurred by evaluating sanitation procedures, the master cleaning schedule, and employee foodhandling practices and training. If necessary, establish new procedures or revise the existing ones.

Providing safe products and conditions also helps keep insurance rates down and, most importantly, ensures a healthy and satisfied clientele. Consumers are increasingly willing to use the law to seek compensation for products that have caused them harm. The Uniform Commercial Code provides an option to people who want compensation for illness or injury caused by unsafe food products. The

plaintiff (the customer) must prove that the food was unfit, that it caused harm, and that in serving unfit food the operator violated the warranty of sale. However, establishments can use a reasonable care defense against a food-related lawsuit. A reasonable care defense requires documented proof that an establishment did everything that could reasonably be expected to ensure that safe food was served. Evidence of written standards, training practices, procedures such as a HACCP plan and its documentation, and positive inspection results are the keys to this defense.

References

1. *ServSafe® Coursebook* ©1999 The Educational Foundation of the National Restaurant Association

Learning Objectives

You will be asked to:

☆ Give examples of foods where microorganisms are most likely to grow.

☆ Identify and classify potentially hazardous foods.

☆ Recognize the name given to the presence of harmful substances.

☆ List the type of storage where microorganisms cannot grow, but cannot be killed.

☆ Describe possible factors responsible for an outbreak of foodborne illness.

☆ Categorize the types of microorganisms that cause foodborne illness and their ideal environment.

Contamination and Spoilage

Contamination is the presence of harmful substances in food. If a food contains any substance that can cause injury or disease to a person who tastes or eats it, that food is contaminated. *Spoilage* is damage to the edible quality of food. Food that has acquired unacceptable taste, appearance, or aroma may be spoiled. The conditions that lead to the spoilage of food are frequently the same that allow pathogenic (disease-causing) microorganisms to flourish. The contaminants may be biological, chemical, or physical, and may be tasteless, odorless, and invisible. Therefore, it is not safe to assume that if the food looks unspoiled it is uncontaminated. Food may show no evident sign that it harbors dangerous microorganisms or toxins.

There are four types of microorganisms that can contaminate food and cause foodborne illness: bacteria, viruses, parasites, and fungi. Except for viruses, all microorganisms need food, water, appropriate temperatures, appropriate oxygen levels, and proper acidity to grow. Bacteria especially can reproduce very rapidly under the right conditions.

Bacteria thrive on proteins and carbohydrates found in food such as meat, poultry, dairy products, and eggs. They grow best in foods that have a neutral pH, or acidity. Most bacteria grow well between the temperatures of 41°F and 140°F (5°C to 60°C). *(See Exhibit 2.1)*. However, refrigeration temperatures may only slow the growth of some bacteria. Additionally, some bacterial spores can survive extreme heat and cold. Most bacteria can grow with or without the presence of oxygen, but most require a moist environment.

Viruses do not require a potentially hazardous food or environment as a medium for transmission. They can be transmitted from person to person, from people to food, and from people to food-contact surfaces. Like some bacteria, some viruses may survive freezing and cooking. They usually contaminate food through a foodhandler's improper personal hygiene. Therefore, practicing good personal hygiene and minimizing hand contact with ready-to-eat foods is an important defense against foodborne viruses.

Parasites are organisms that require a living host—a person, animal, or plant, on which it can live and take nourishment. Most are typically passed to humans through an animal host and may be killed by proper cooking or freezing.

Fungi include molds and yeasts and are found naturally in air, soil, plants, animals, water, and some foods. Both grow well in sweet, acidic foods with low water activity such as cheeses, breads, and jellies. Freezing temperatures prevent or reduce the growth of mold but do not destroy it. Foods that have been spoiled by mold or yeast should always be discarded. (Some molds are a natural part of certain food products such as cheeses like Gorgonzola, Bleu cheese, Brie, and Camembert. These are specific types of molds which are grown in very specific and controlled conditions.)

Foodborne Illness

A *foodborne illness* is a disease that is carried or transmitted to humans by food. An outbreak is defined as an incident in which two or more people experience the same illness after eating the same food, which is confirmed through laboratory analysis as the source of the illness. While there are some foods that present more risk than others, any kind of food can be a vehicle for foodborne illness.

The following is a list of the eight most frequently cited factors involved in outbreaks of foodborne illness.

☐ Food is not heated or cooked thoroughly.

☐ Food is not cooled quickly and thoroughly.

☐ Infected employees practice poor personal hygiene.

☐ Foods are prepared a day or more before they are served.

☐ Raw, contaminated ingredients mix with foods that receive no further cooking.

☐ Foods remain at temperatures that encourage microorganism growth.

☐ Previously cooked foods are not reheated to temperatures that kill bacteria.

☐ Cross-contamination between cooked foods and raw ingredients occurs when workers mishandle foods, when food is improperly stored, or when equipment is improperly cleaned.

Potentially Hazardous Foods

Some of the foods implicated in foodborne illnesses are poisonous by nature, such as certain types of mushrooms. However, it is primarily high-protein and low-acid foods—poultry, red meats, fish, dairy products, and eggs—that are responsible for most foodborne illnesses. Such foods are receptive hosts to certain forms of bacteria and other disease agents. These high-protein foods are classified as potentially hazardous by the FDA Model Food Code, which identifies potentially hazardous food as any food that consists in whole or in part of:

☐ Milk or milk products

☐ Shell eggs

☐ Meats, poultry, and fish

☐ Shellfish and edible crustacea (such as shrimp, lobster, crab)

☐ Baked or boiled potatoes

☐ Tofu or other soy-protein foods

☐ Garlic and oil mixtures

☐ Plant foods that have been heat-treated (cooked, partially cooked, or warmed)

☐ Raw seeds and sprouts

☐ Sliced melons

☐ Synthetic ingredients (such as textured soy protein in hamburger supplement)

Poor storage, preparation, and service worsen the problem. Potentially hazardous foods may become contaminated if handled incorrectly at any stage in the flow of the food. Identifying potentially hazardous foods and understanding how they need to be handled is especially important because they are known to support the rapid growth of pathogens that cause foodborne illness.

References

1. *ServSafe® Coursebook* ©1999 The Educational Foundation of the National Restaurant Association

Learning Objectives

You will be asked to:

☆ State the temperature range where microorganisms will most likely grow and multiply.

☆ Select the stage of food-preparation that kills most disease-causing microorganisms.

☆ List the consequences of failing to heat, cook, and cool food thoroughly.

☆ Choose and explain the best reason for establishing a HACCP system.

☆ Distinguish the difference between a critical control point and a critical limit.

☆ Identify the correct temperature ranges for holding hot foods and cold foods.

☆ State the correct temperature of the refrigerator air that will keep food at its maximum safe storage temperature.

☆ Given a list of food items, determine where they need to be placed within a refrigerator.

☆ Identify the most common problems of dry storerooms.

☆ State which methods prevent cross-contamination during food-preparation.

☆ Specify the minimum internal cooking temperature of most foods.

☆ List correct methods when using a microwave oven to thaw and cook foods.

☆ Describe appropriate action in dealing with food that has been cooled from 140°F to 90°F (60°C to 31°C) in a two-hour period.

☆ Identify situations when food needs to be discarded.

Keeping Food Safe from Storage to Service

Temperature Abuse

Potentially the biggest factor in outbreaks of foodborne illness is temperature abuse. Disease-causing microorganisms grow and multiply in temperatures between 41°F and 140°F (5°C and 60°C), which is why this range is known as the temperature danger zone. Microorganisms grow much faster in the middle of the zone, at temperatures between 70°F and 120°F. Whenever food is held in the temperature danger zone, it is being temperature abused. *(See Exhibit 2.1.)*

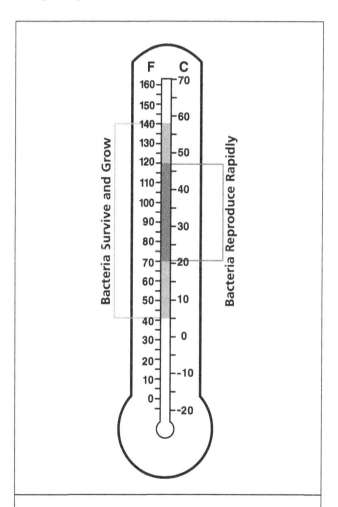

Exhibit 2.1
Temperature and Bacterial Growth. Most microorganisms grow rapidly at temperatures between 70°F and 120°F (21°C and 49°C).

Microorganisms need both time and temperature to reproduce and grow. The longer food stays in the temperature danger zone, the more time microorganisms have to multiply. When heating or cooling foods, it is important to pass them through the danger zone as quickly and as few times as possible.

Storing Food Safely

Every establishment needs to store food and supplies. How and where food is stored affects food quality and safety. All foods lose quality over time. They may contain high levels of illness-causing microorganisms long before they appear unfit to eat. Proper storage techniques can help preserve food quality and safety. Poor storage practices can cause food to spoil quickly, with potentially serious results. Remember, when in doubt, throw it out.

A few general rules can be applied to most storage situations:

☐ Use the first in, first out FIFO method.

☐ Keep potentially hazardous foods out of the temperature danger zone.

☐ Check temperatures of stored foods and storage areas.

☐ Wrap foods tightly in clean, moisture-proof containers.

☐ Keep all storage areas clean and dry.

☐ Store foods only in areas designed for them.

Food items purchased in unsealed containers should be transferred to airtight containers to protect them from insects and vermin. Proper sanitation and cleanliness are essential at all times. Storage areas must be cleaned and swept daily to eliminate spoiled foods and to discourage insect and vermin infestation.

A key factor in storing foods, especially perishables, is temperature. When temperatures rise above specific levels, most foods' shelf life decreases and the incidence of waste and spoilage increases. Refrigerated storage generally ranges from 32°F to 41°F, or -1°C to 7°C. *(See Exhibit 2.2.)* Dry storage

areas should be kept between 50°F and 75°F (10°C and 24°C), while frozen storage areas must hold food below 0°F (-18°C).

Refrigerated Storage. In general, the colder food is, the safer it is. Ideal storage temperatures will vary depending on the food. *(See Exhibit 2.2.)* To hold food at a certain temperature, refrigerator air temperature needs to be at least 2°-3°F (1°C) lower than the desired temperature. For example, to hold poultry at a safe internal temperature of 41°F (5°C), the air temperature in the refrigerator needs to be 38°F (3°C).

Monitor food temperatures regularly. Use caution when chilling large quantities of hot food in the refrigerator. This can warm up the interior enough to put other foods into the temperature danger zone. For maximum efficiency, do not overload refrigerator units and use open shelving to allow for maximum circulation of cold air. Keep the door closed as much as possible. Cool foods in shallow containers, uncovered, on the top shelf. When cooled, products should be stored in clean, covered food containers with clearly marked labels.

There is a new generation of refrigerated food that has special characteristics and special requirements for receiving and storage. These foods include refrigerated entrées, prepared salads, fresh pasta, soups, sauces and gravies, cooked or partially cured meats, and poultry dishes. Other terms sometimes used for these new-generation foods include fresh-prepared foods, fresh-refrigerated foods, and ready-to-eat chilled foods. These items may be packaged under vacuum (called *sous vide*) or with a mix of gases inside (called *modified atmosphere packaging* or *MAP*) to extend shelf life. Always follow manufacturer instructions for storage temperatures of specially packaged foods.

Store raw meat, poultry, and fish separately from cooked and ready-to-eat foods whenever possible. If this is not possible, then store prepared or ready-to-eat foods above raw meat, poultry, and fish. This will prevent raw product juices from dripping on, and potentially contaminating, the prepared

Food	Recommended Temperatures	Maximum Storage Periods	Comments
Meat			
Roasts, steaks, chops	35-41°F (2-5°C)	2-5 days	Wrap loosely
Steaks	35-41°F (2-5°C)	2-5 days	Wrap loosely
Chops	35-41°F (2-5°C)	3-4 days	Wrap loosely
Ground and stewing	35-41°F (2-5°C)	1-2 days	Wrap loosely
Variety meats	35-41°F (2-5°C)	1-2 days	Wrap loosely
Whole ham	35-41°F (2-5°C)	7 days	May wrap tightly
Half ham	35-41°F (2-5°C)	3-5 days	May wrap tightly
Ham slices	35-41°F (2-5°C)	3-5 days	May wrap tightly
Canned ham	35-41°F (2-5°C)	9 months to 1 year	
Frankfurters	35-41°F (2-5°C)	1 week	
Bacon	35-41°F (2-5°C)	5-7 days unopened	May wrap tightly
Luncheon meats	35-41°F (2-5°C)	3-5 days	Wrap tightly after opening
Leftover cooked meats	35-41°F (2-5°C)	1-2 days	Wrap or cover tightly
Gravy, broth	35-41°F (2-5°C)	1-2 days	Cover
Poultry			
Whole bird	32-36°F (0-2°C)	1-2 days	Wrap loosely
Giblets	32-36°F (0-2°C)	1-2 days	Wrap separate from bird
Cooked stuffing	32-36°F (0-2°C)	1 day	In a covered container, separate from bird
Cut-up cooked poultry	32-36°F (0-2°C)	1-2 days	Cover
Fish			
Fresh fish	32-36°F (0-2°C)	1-2 days	Wrap loosely
Fish (smoked)	30-41°F (-1-5°C)	1-2 days	Wrap loosely
Clams, crab, lobster (in shell)	30-41°F (-1-5°C)	2 days	Cover
Scallops, oysters, shrimp	30-41°F (-1-5°C)	1 day	Cover
New Generation Foods			
Sous vide packaged foods			Follow manufacturer's instructions
MAP (Modified atmosphere packaged foods)			Follow manufacturer's instructions
Eggs			
Eggs in shell	45°F (7°C)	*4-5 weeks beyond pack date	Do not wash
Leftover yolks	40-45°F (4-7°C)	1-2 days	Cover yolks with water
Leftover whites	40-45°F (4-7°C)	4 days	
Dried eggs (whole eggs and yolks)	40-45°F (4-7°C)	Up to 1 year (unreconstituted)	
Reconstituted dried eggs			Use immediately
Dairy Products			
Fluid milk	35-41°F (2-5°C)	5-7 days after date on container	Keep covered in original container
Butter	35-41°F (2-5°C)	2 weeks	Waxed cartons
Hard cheese (cheddar, parmesan, romano)	35-41°F (2-5°C)	1 month	Cover tightly
Soft cheese	35-41°F (2-5°C)	1 week	Cover tightly
Reconstituted dry milk	35-41°F (2-5°C)	5-7 days	Treat as fluid milk
Cooked dishes with eggs, meat, milk, fish, poultry	32-36°F (0-2°C)	1 day	Highly perishable; serve the day they are prepared
Fruit			Varies according to ripeness and geographic location
Vegetables			
Artichokes, asparagus, broccoli, carrots, cauliflower, celery, corn, lettuce, mushrooms, pea	32-35°F (0-2°C)	Varies	Most are highly perishable even at refrigerated temperatures
Beans, cucumbers, eggplant, peppers	45-50°F (7-10°C)	Varies	Most are very perishable at room temperature

*Recommended by the American Egg Board. Most eggs arrive at a distribution site within a few days of being packed.

Exhibit 2.2
Guidelines for Proper Refrigerated Storage

foods. Store raw meat, poultry, and fish in vertical order based on the minimum internal cooking temperature of each food. Foods with the highest minimum internal cooking temperature should be placed at the lowest shelves of the refrigerator. These foods should be stored, from the bottom shelf up, in the following order: poultry; ground beef and ground pork; pork, bacon, ham, and sausage; whole cuts of beef; fish. *(See Exhibit 2.3.)*

Freezer and Dry Storage. Keep freezer temperatures at 0°F (-18°C) or below unless different foods require different temperatures. Open the unit as infrequently as possible. Place frozen food deliveries in freezers as soon as they have been inspected. Defrost freezer units on a regular basis. Never refreeze thawed food unless it has been thoroughly cooked.

Storerooms for dry foods should be clean and dry. They should be well ventilated to minimize moisture and heat—the biggest problems in dry

Exhibit 2.3
Refrigerator Storage of Raw and Prepared Foods in the Same Refrigerator.

storerooms. The temperature of the storeroom should be between 50°F and 70°F (10°C to 21°C). Keep relative humidity at around 50 or 60 percent. Store dry foods at least six inches off the floor, away from walls, and out of direct sunlight in their original packages or in tightly covered containers. Clean up any spills in the storeroom immediately.

Handling Food Safely

All food must be handled safely at every step of the process. Food-preparation procedures must be tightly controlled to ensure that the following takes place.

☐ Foods are not subjected to temperatures in which bacteria grow and multiply most rapidly (41°F to 140°F, or 5°C to 60°C) for longer than four hours. *(See Exhibit 2.1.)*

☐ Foodhandlers practice good personal hygiene as a critical protective measure against contaminating food and possibly causing foodborne illness.

☐ Any surface that comes in contact with food must be cleaned and sanitized after each use to prevent cross-contamination.

☐ Raw meats, fish, and poultry are prepared in separate areas from produce or cooked and ready-to-eat foods to prevent cross-contamination.

☐ Specific containers are used for each type of food product and are cleaned and sanitized between uses to prevent cross-contamination.

☐ Cloths or towels used for wiping food spills must not be used for any other purpose. Use disposable towels or rinse and store cloths or towels in a clean sanitizing solution after each use.

If frozen foods are thawed improperly, they can become breeding grounds for microorganisms. There are four acceptable methods of thawing foods:

☐ Place frozen food in the refrigerator at temperatures of 41°F (5°C) or less.

☐ Submerge the frozen product in running potable water at a temperature of 70°F (21°C) or below. Make sure that the thawed product does not drip water onto other products or surfaces. Clean and sanitize the sink and work area before and after thawing food this way.

☐ Use a microwave oven only if food is to be cooked immediately afterward.

☐ Cook the food, making sure that the minimum internal cooking temperature is achieved. *(See Exhibit 2.4.)*

The utensils that foodhandlers use also play an important role in keeping food safe. Utensils should have long handles and can be stored in the food with the handle extended above the rim of the container. Utensils should be used for only one food and must be properly cleaned and sanitized after each task, or at least once every four hours during continuous use.

Care must be taken when handling ready-to-eat foods, which may also be considered unsafe because they are intended to be eaten without further washing or cooking. Proper cooking reduces the number of microorganisms on food to safe levels. Foods that have been properly cooked and washed fruits and vegetables (whole or cut) are considered ready-to-eat foods.

Principles of Safe Cooking

A good understanding of all cooking methods will help insure quality results and add appeal to a menu. Special care should be taken when cooking fruits and vegetables. It is best to choose the cooking method that will enhance their flavor and texture. Likewise, different cooking methods are suited to different cuts of meat. Broiling, for example, enhances the flavor of steaks or ground meat that has an ample amount of fat to keep it moist, but would dry out a brisket.

Whatever cooking method you choose, temperature is key to killing microorganisms that can cause illness. The internal temperature of the product must reach a certain level for a specific amount of time before the number of microorganisms in the food has been sufficiently reduced. The minimum internal temperature at which microorganisms are destroyed varies from product to product. In general, foods should be cooked to an internal temperature of at least 145°F (63°C) for at least fifteen seconds, though some foods must reach an internal temperature of 165°F (74°C). *(See Exhibit 2.4.)*

Microwave ovens tend to cook food more unevenly than other methods of cooking. For this reason, there are special rules for using microwave ovens:

☐ Rotate or stir food halfway through the cooking process to distribute heat more evenly.

☐ Cover food to prevent the surface from drying out.

Product	Temperature
Poultry, stuffing, stuffed meats, stuffed pasta, casseroles, field-dressed game	165°F (74°C) for 15 seconds
Pork, ham, bacon, injected meats	145°F (63°C) for 15 seconds
Ground or flaked meats including hamburger, ground pork, flaked fish, ground game animals, sausage, gyros	155°F (69°C) for 15 seconds
Beef and pork roasts (rare)	145°F (63°C) for 3 minutes
Beef steaks, veal, lamb, commercially raised game animals	145°F (63°C) for 15 seconds
Fish	145°F (63°C) for 15 seconds
Shell eggs for immediate service	145°F (63°C) for 15 seconds
Any potentially hazardous food cooked in a microwave oven	165°F (74°C); let food stand for 2 minutes after cooking

Exhibit 2.4
Minimum Safe Internal Cooking Temperatures

☐ Let food stand after cooking for at least two minutes to allow product temperature to equalize.

Meat, poultry, or fish cooked in a microwave oven must be heated to 165°F (74°C) or above. Check the internal temperature of the food in several places to make sure it has cooked through.

When preparing recipes calling for eggs, special care must be taken to ensure safe production. For instance, raw eggs should never be pooled (mixing unprepared raw with prepared raw quantities in advance of cooking) because of the unacceptably long time the eggs may be left in dangerous temperatures. Also, one contaminated egg will contaminate all others. Freshly prepared eggs should never be mixed with eggs that have been held, and scrambled eggs should always be cooked to above 140°F (60°C) and to a firm texture. In addition, use pasteurized eggs in recipes calling for uncooked or lightly cooked eggs, such as hollandaise sauce and Caesar salad dressing. Pasteurized eggs should always be used when serving susceptible populations such as young children, the elderly, or persons with weakened immune systems.

Cooling and Reheating Methods

The FDA Model Food Code recommends a two-stage cooling method. By this method, cooked foods must be cooled from 140°F (60°C) to 70°F (21°C) within two hours and from 70°F (21°C) to below 41°F (5°C) in an additional four hours for a total cooling time of six hours. Some jurisdictions, however, follow the one-stage, four-hour method by which foods must be cooled to 41°F (5°C) or lower in less than four hours total after cooking or hot holding.

When using the two-stage cooling method, if the food has not reached 70°F (21°C) within two hours, the food must be reheated. Reheat the food to 165°F (74°C) for fifteen seconds within two hours, or throw it out. Re-evaluate your cooling methods if they are consistently inadequate.

When previously cooked food is reheated for hot holding, it must be reheated to an internal temperature of 165°F (74°C) for fifteen seconds within two hours of its original cooking time. Never mix leftover foods with freshly prepared foods. When adding previously cooked food as an ingredient to another food, such as adding ground beef to spaghetti sauce, the whole mixture must be reheated to 165°F (74°C).

Follow the same rules for microwave cooking when using the microwave oven to reheat previously cooked foods. Foods that are reheated for immediate issue, such as a roast beef sandwich, may be served at any temperature as long as the beef was properly cooked and not subjected to dangerous temperatures before reheating. If properly cooked food that has cooled is not reheated to 165°F (74°C) within two hours, throw it out.

Holding Foods

Microbial growth may occur if previously cooked food is held or displayed for long periods of time. The best policy is to avoid preparing too much food or preparing food too far in advance. If this is not possible, keep food that already has a temperature of at least 140°F (60°C) at that temperature.

Never use hot-holding equipment to reheat previously cooked foods. Reheat the food first to 165°F (74°C) and then transfer it to holding equipment. Use only hot-holding equipment that can keep foods at 140°F (60°C) or higher. Stir foods at regular intervals to distribute heat evenly throughout the food and keep food covered. Measure the internal food temperature at least every two hours with a probe thermometer. Remember, the thermostat of the holding equipment measures the temperature of the equipment, not of the food.

Prepare hot food in small batches so it will be used faster. Never mix freshly prepared food with foods being held for service. Discard hot foods after four hours if they have not been held at or above 140°F (60°C).

For holding cold foods, use only cold-holding equipment that can keep foods at 41°F (5°C) or less. Other than whole fruits and vegetables and raw cut vegetables, most foods should not be stored directly on ice. If ice is to be used on a display, it should be self-draining and the drip pans need to be washed and sanitized after each use. Measure internal temperatures at least every two hours and discard food that has not been consistently held at 41°F (5°C). Protect cold food from contaminants with covers or food shields.

HACCP

Hazard Analysis Critical Control Point (HACCP) food safety systems combine up-to-date technical information with step-by-step procedures to evaluate and monitor the flow of food—from receiving to serving—through an establishment. A HACCP system helps a foodservice operation:

☐ Identify foods, hazards, and processes most likely to cause foodborne illnesses.

☐ Develop control points through the flow of food to reduce risks of foodborne illness outbreaks.

☐ Set critical limits.

☐ Monitor and verify food safety.

The following are the seven principles of any HACCP system:

1. Identify and Assess Food Safety Hazards. The process of identifying and evaluating potential hazards associated with foods is key to determining where hazards may occur in the flow of food if extra care is not taken to prevent or control them.

2. Identify Critical Control Points (CCPs). A control point is any step in the flow of food where a physical, chemical, or biological hazard can be controlled. To assess whether a control point is critical, determine if it is the last step where microorganism growth can be prevented, controlled, or eliminated before the food is served to customers. Cooking, cooling, or holding foods are typically named CCPs. However, these may not be the CCPs for all foods or processes in an establishment. Each situation must be evaluated on an individual basis.

3. Establish Critical Limits for CCPs. Critical limits are minimum and maximum standards that a CCP must meet in order to prevent, eliminate, or reduce a hazard to an acceptable limit.

4. Set Up Procedures to Monitor CCPs. Develop clear directions that will determine how the CCP will be monitored, when and how often it will be monitored, and who and what (equipment, tools, materials) will monitor it. Monitoring lets you know that critical limits are being met.

5. Take Corrective Actions. Specific and immediate actions must be established to correct food-safety errors as they occur. Corrective actions are predetermined steps taken when food doesn't meet a critical limit.

6. Verify That the System Works. Verify that the CCPs and critical limits are appropriate, that monitoring alerts you to hazards, that corrective actions are adequate to prevent foodborne illness from occurring, and that employees are following established procedures.

7. Set Up a Record-Keeping System. Proper records provide documentation that safe food is continuously being prepared and served.

HACCP flowcharts and the identification of CCP's will vary among food items and operations. They will include a combination of proper food handling procedures, monitoring techniques, and record keeping so that the likelihood of food remaining safe through each step in the process is maximized.

Training is critical in making a HACCP plan successful. HACCP works best when it is integrated into each employee's job description and duties.

References

1. *A Practical Approach to HACCP Coursebook* ©1998 The Educational Foundation of the National Restaurant Association

2. *ServSafe® Coursebook* ©1999 The Educational Foundation of the National Restaurant Association

Sanitation

Proper sanitation is fundamental to all establishments regardless of size or complexity of operation.

Clean vs. Sanitary

While *clean* means free of visible soil, *sanitary* means free of disease-causing organisms and other harmful contaminants. Clean refers to aesthetics and outward appearances—a smudge-free dish, a sparkling glass, a shelf wiped clear of dust. However, these objects, though clean on the surface, can harbor invisible disease-causing agents or harmful chemicals. Sanitary means that the object is free from harmful levels of disease-causing organisms and other harmful contamination.

Sanitation-conscious managers will keep both of these concepts in mind and operate their establishments by the rule: Look clean—be sanitary.

Training Employees

Ensuring safe food is a matter of implementing and maintaining good sanitary practices in food purchasing, storage, and preparation. Training employees in sanitary practices is a key factor. Employees should be trained before unsanitary habits develop—beginning the first day on the job. A combination of training techniques and materials is the best approach for sanitation training.

Sanitation policies should be based on the principles of good personal hygiene. Good personal hygiene is key to the prevention of foodborne illness. Good personal hygiene includes:

☐ Hygienic hand practices

☐ Maintaining personal cleanliness

☐ Wearing clean and appropriate uniforms and following dress codes

☐ Avoiding unsanitary habits and actions

☐ Maintaining good health

☐ Reporting illnesses

Establishments should implement strict policies regarding eating, drinking, smoking, and chewing gum and tobacco. In the process of any of these activities, small droplets of saliva that can contain thousands of disease-causing microorganisms can be transferred to the foodhandler's hands or to the food they are handling. For this reason, managers need to strictly enforce such policies.

Many local health services serve as consultants on safe foodhandling practices and provide help with employee training. They often also advise operators on meeting requirements for sanitary facilities.

To ensure effective training and consistent adherence to sanitation policies, employees must see that the commitment to sanitation and food safety comes from the top down. Management should lead by example. If managers show a commitment to food safety and sanitation in their behavior and attitude, employees are likely to follow.

Good Personal Hygiene

Personal hygiene can be a sensitive subject for some people, but because it is vital to food safety, it must be addressed with every employee. A successful personal hygiene program depends on trained foodhandlers who possess the knowledge, skills, and attitude necessary to maintain a safe food system.

While it may appear fundamental, many foodhandlers fail to wash their hands properly and as often as needed. It is a manager's responsibility to train his foodhandlers and then monitor them to make sure that they are washing their hands properly and when necessary. Never take this single action for granted. Foodhandlers must wash their hands thoroughly:

- ☐ After using the restroom.
- ☐ Before and after handling raw foods.
- ☐ After touching the hair, face, or body.
- ☐ After sneezing, coughing, or using a handkerchief or tissue.

- ☐ After smoking, eating, drinking, or chewing gum or tobacco.
- ☐ After using any cleaning, polishing, or sanitizing chemical.
- ☐ After taking out garbage or trash.
- ☐ After clearing tables or busing dirty dishes.
- ☐ After touching clothing or aprons.
- ☐ After touching anything else that may contaminate hands, such as unsanitized equipment, work surfaces, or wash cloths.

Gloves can help ensure food safety by creating a barrier between hands and food. Tongs or other utensils, or barriers such as deli tissue can also be used to protect food. However, these items must never be used as substitutes for handwashing. When practiced and reinforced, proper hand sanitation can become a lifetime habit that will help prevent foodborne illness.

Any cuts, burns, boils, sores, skin infections, or infected wounds should be covered with a bandage when a foodhandler is working with or around food or food-contact surfaces. Waterproof disposable gloves or finger cots should be worn over bandages on hands.

Proper work attire also plays an important role in the prevention of foodborne illness. Foodhandlers should remove jewelry prior to preparing or serving food or while around food-preparation areas. Foodhandlers should wear a clean hat or other hair restraint and their clothing should be clean. Their shoes should be clean as well, with a closed-toe and a sensible, non-slip sole. Foodhandlers should also remove their aprons when leaving food-preparation areas.

Management plays a critical role in the effectiveness of sanitary practices. By establishing a program that includes specific policies, and by training and reinforcing those policies, managers can minimize the risk of causing foodborne illness.

Reporting Employee Illnesses

Foodhandlers must report health problems to the manager before working with food. According to the FDA Model Food Code, managers must exclude from the establishment foodhandlers who have been diagnosed with a foodborne illness and notify the local regulatory agency. Managers are also responsible for prohibiting foodhandlers from working with or around food if they have symptoms that include diarrhea, jaundice (yellow skin and eyes), vomiting, fever, or sore throat. Managers must work with local regulatory agencies to determine when foodhandlers can safely return to work.

References

1. *ServSafe® Coursebook* ©1999 The Educational Foundation of the National Restaurant Association

<table>
<tr><td>

Learning Objectives

You will be asked to:

☆ Relate appropriate action in a foodborne illness complaint case.

☆ Outline key steps in determining whether a customer complaint is directly related to the food he or she was served.

</td></tr>
</table>

Responding to an Outbreak of Foodborne Illness

Despite the best of efforts, an outbreak of foodborne illness can occur in any establishment at any time. Responding quickly to customers' complaints may avert a crisis. Take all customer complaints seriously. Express concern and be sincere, but do not admit responsibility or accept liability. Listen carefully and promise to investigate and respond. To help identify the illness and determine whether your food is the cause, write down all facts about the incident.

If the complaint is isolated, use it as an opportunity to review food-safety procedures with employees. Remind them of the importance of good personal hygiene. If you have a HACCP system in place, review all documentation on the date in question and verify that the system was and is working. Pay close attention to temperature and equipment issues.

If more than one person has complained, contact your local health department. Remember that an outbreak of foodborne illness is defined as an incident in which laboratory tests have confirmed the complaints of two people who have experienced similar symptoms after eating the same food. Health department officials can help you determine the cause and source of the foodborne illness. They can also act as an information resource for the media.

If you have received more than two complaints, you may have a crisis on your hands. However, you can minimize potential damage by taking the following steps:

☐ Assemble your crisis team to gather information, plan courses of action, and manage events as they unfold.

☐ Appoint a single spokesperson to handle all media inquiries and communications.

☐ Work with, not against the media.

☐ Develop a communication system to get information directly to all of your key audiences.

☐ Fix the problem and communicate what you've done both to the media and to your customers.

References

1. *ServSafe® Coursebook* ©1999 The Educational Foundation of the National Restaurant Association

Learning Objectives

You will be asked to:

☆ Identify and give examples of effective waste management procedures.

☆ State the best method of pest prevention.

☆ Recommend appropriate action to comply with waste management and recycling ordinances.

Waste Management

Waste management involves a number of important aspects of a foodservice operation: sanitation, pest control, waste disposal, recycling, and adherence to a variety of local and federal regulations and laws.

Solid waste is dry, bulky trash that includes glass bottles, plastic wrappers and containers, paper bags, and cardboard boxes. *Garbage* is wet waste, usually from food, that may become a hazard to a foodservice operation because it attracts pests and can contaminate food items, equipment, and utensils. Some rules for handling garbage are as follows.

☐ Never allow garbage to accumulate inside or outside.

☐ Remove all garbage as soon as possible from food-preparation areas.

☐ Use appropriate containers.

☐ Store outside containers on or above a smooth surface.

☐ Keep containers tightly covered.

☐ Keep all garbage in a designated area.

☐ Provide an area to clean containers.

☐ Clean containers frequently and thoroughly.

Establish procedures for waste management and recycling based on these rules and monitor employees to see that they are followed.

There are several types of equipment that can reduce the volume of waste—pulpers, grinders, and mechanical compactors. One method for dealing with trash is *source reduction*—decreasing the total amount of material received or used, and thus, decreasing the total amount of material disposed. For example, eliminate unnecessary packaging, such as multiple layers of overwrap.

Recycling is another method of dealing with waste. Recycling involves separating and storing recyclable items for pickup. When you recycle, you have to exercise caution in the storage of these materials so that they don't attract pests. Check local regulations for recommendations or requirements for storage and handling of recyclables.

Using these systems greatly reduces the need for landfills. Environment-conscious managers can take the following steps to help solve the solid waste problem:

☐ Train your employees to eliminate unnecessary waste.

☐ Evaluate the packaging of the products received by your operation.

☐ Initiate a source reduction recycling program in your operation.

☐ Participate in local recycling programs.

☐ Join with other operators to identify a hauler who will take recyclables to recycling centers.

Pests such as insects and rodents can pose serious problems for establishments. Integrated pest management (IPM) is a program that uses prevention and control measures to contain or eliminate a pest infestation in an establishment. There are three basic rules of an IPM program:

1. Deny pests access to the facility. Check all deliveries before they enter the facility and refuse any shipment in which you find pests or signs of infestation.

2. Deny pests food, water, and a hiding or nesting place. Garbage removal and thorough sanitizing will reduce the number of places pests can take shelter.

3. Work with a licensed pest control operator to eliminate pests that do enter.

References

1. *ServSafe® Coursebook* ©1999 The Educational Foundation of the National Restaurant Association

Learning Objectives

You will be asked to:

☆ Describe the role of Occupational Safety and Health Administration (OSHA).

☆ State when OSHA reports need to be filed.

☆ Explain the general provisions of workers' compensation benefits.

Safety and Security

Foodservice operators as a whole have become increasingly aware of their responsibility—and possible liability—for their customers and employees. Foodservice security involves issues that are both internal (employees) and external (customers) in nature. Because foodservice operations are open to the public, and because inventory supplies and even cash are often accessible to employees, security is an important part of foodservice management. These issues affect important financial, legal, and service aspects of an operation.

Public and Employee Liability

Customers of foodservice establishments have a legal right to expect safe food served in a safe environment on safe premises. Employees also have a legal right to work in a safe environment that is free of hazards. Establishments that fail to provide safety for their customers or employees can be sued and can lose their good reputation as well as large sums of money.

An establishment's responsibility to customers includes both public and product liability. Public liability covers everyone who has a legitimate reason to be on the premises, such as employees, guests, and vendors. Also covered are members of the general public who are injured through the actions of employees working away from the premises, for example, delivery personnel. Product liability involves a restaurant being held liable for any ill effects a customer may suffer from the food it serves, even if negligence is not a factor. Managers are expected to know about hazards, do whatever is necessary to correct them, and be sure there are proper warnings where everyone can see them. If an accident does happen, the court may hold restaurants legally responsible, citing a number of doctrines and practices.

Worker's Compensation was designed to provide relief for employees who were injured in occupational accidents or made ill by job-related conditions. Worker's Compensation provides cash benefits, payments for medical treatment, and payments for rehabilitation and retraining. In return, the employee generally gives up the right to sue the employer—a practice known as *exclusive remedy*. In most states, employers—including foodservice operations—are required to purchase workers' compensation coverage for their employees. Generally, the courts have held restaurants, and most other employers, to standards of employee responsibility stricter than those applied to customer liability.

The Occupational Safety and Health Administration (OSHA) is the United States governmental agency that creates and enforces safety-related standards and regulations in the workplace. OSHA has specific documentation standards and forms for investigating and reporting accidents, injuries, and illnesses. Any accident resulting in death or the hospitalization of five or more employees must be reported to OSHA within 48 hours.

OSHA may inspect any operation to ensure compliance with safety standards. To determine which operations to inspect, OSHA has established a system of inspection priorities based on imminent danger, multiple hospitalization and fatal accidents, and employee complaints. Inspectors are likely to check each part of your hazard communication program. The most common OSHA violation in foodservice establishments is the absence of a hazard communication program.

References

1. Workplace Safety Program, which consists of the following five titles: *Designing and Implementing a Safety Program; Preventing Burns; Preventing Cuts; Preventing Lifting and Carrying Injuries;* and *Preventing Slips, Trips, and Falls* © 1999 The Educational Foundation of the National Restaurant Association

Learning Objectives

You will be asked to:

☆ Identify key components in any establishment's HCS.

☆ Define the purpose of a HCS.

☆ Distinguish between a physical hazard and a health hazard.

The Hazard Communication Standard (HCS)

HCS, also called "Right-to-Know" and "HAZCOM," requires that all employers notify their employees about chemical hazards present on the job, and train employees to use these materials safely.

Chemicals may be physical hazards, health hazards, or both. *Physical hazards* are those that could cause property damage and immediate injury due to chemicals that are flammable, explosive, highly reactive to air or water, or stored under pressure. *Health hazards* cause long- or short-term injuries or illnesses. Chemicals that are toxic, carcinogenic, irritating, or corrosive are considered to be health hazards.

The following are required components in a restaurant's HCS:

☐ A written policy stating the establishment's intention to comply with OSHA requirements.

☐ An up-to-date, written list of every chemical product stored and used at the establishment, including product name and its location in the establishment.

☐ A Material Safety Data Sheet (MSDS) for each chemical on the inventory list. MSDS's describe the hazards of the chemicals in an operation and are usually supplied by the manufacturer or supplier. Each product has it own MSDS.

☐ A written description of the labels that will be used on all chemical containers.

☐ Easy-to-read labels on each chemical container.

☐ A written copy of the establishment's training program for employees.

References

1. Workplace Safety Program, which consists of the following five titles: *Designing and Implementing a Safety Program; Preventing Burns; Preventing Cuts; Preventing Lifting and Carrying Injuries;* and *Preventing Slips, Trips, and Falls* © 1999 The Educational Foundation of the National Restaurant Association

Learning Objectives

You will be asked to:

☆ Recommend what elements should be included in written safety procedures.

☆ Choose when new employees should be trained in safety.

☆ Distinguish between a physical hazard and a health hazard.

☆ Describe the composition of an emergency response team.

☆ Specify when to establish an emergency response team.

☆ Identify an effective emergency plan.

A Safety Program

A safety program can control risk, lower operating costs, and increase profitability. It helps managers provide reasonable care, and offers written evidence that reasonable care was provided. By actively involving all employees in safety procedures and programs, and by letting them know their well-being is a management priority, you will help increase their job satisfaction which can, in turn, reduce turnover and accident-related expenses.

Developing a Safety Program

The first step in developing a safety program is to review existing records on accidents, injuries, repairs, and insurance claims to determine if a pattern exists. Examine the types of accidents that have occurred as well as their frequency and severity. Slips, falls, cuts, and burns are among the types of accidents commonly reported in the industry. This review will determine the priorities of the program. Consult with your insurance carrier, attorney, and vendors for additional information on developing a program.

The next step is to list the areas that are or might be hazardous to employees and customers. The purpose of this audit is to give you an overview of the level of safety in an establishment. The general areas covered in a safety audit are facilities, equipment, employee practices, and management commitment to protect employees and customers. A program should satisfy the particular needs of the operation. For instance, an establishment in San Francisco may require structural provisions in case of an earthquake while an establishment in New Orleans may require safety procedures in the event of a hurricane.

Develop policy statements based on the size of your establishment, number of employees, and whether your establishment is corporate or local. Write a mission statement defining the purpose of the safety program. State the scope, which includes all areas covered in the program. Finally, identify the job positions with overall authority for the program and state their responsibilities. Assess your employees' capabilities and experience and then assign appropriate tasks.

Documenting and Monitoring a Safety Program

Hazardous job policies and procedures should focus on what to do, how to do it, and the steps to complete the task correctly. Written procedures are an important part of documentation and training. Whenever possible, involve employees in developing procedures, reviewing their job responsibilities, and conducting safety audits.

Plan for weekly, monthly, or quarterly meetings to emphasize safety issues and resolve specific problems. Meetings can be scheduled for the entire employee group or for individual teams or shifts. Use the meetings to focus on one or two specific topics. Keep the meeting positive and use it to reinforce your safety commitment. Avoid openly criticizing employees.

Regular safety self-inspections are an effective way to bridge employees' safety training and on-the-job behavior. Scheduled and unscheduled safety inspections allow you to review employees' safety practices and produce detailed records of your establishment's safety efforts. Checklists will ensure that inspections are carried out and reported to management.

Any event that compromises customer or employee safety should be investigated and recorded in an annual log of injuries and illnesses, even if an injury did not occur. Study the data in the log by specific areas of operation, such as the exterior, kitchen, or dining areas. Considering the time of day and seasons of the year as well as certain employee jobs and levels of experience may assist in identifying changing needs of the safety program.

Safety Training

Training is an essential element of your safety program because it gives employees the information and skills to protect themselves from injuries. The purpose of safety training and specific job instruction is to provide employees with an understanding of the role safety has in preventing accidents and injuries and in helping increase profits. Training is necessary when you hire new employees and introduce new equipment, menu items, and products.

Overall, training should be as practical as possible—employees do not need to memorize extensive safety methods and terms, but they should retain what they have learned. Establish training priorities based on your safety program. Specific topics to consider for your training program may include:

☐ Ensuring fire safety.

☐ Proper handling and use of foodservice chemicals.

☐ Preventing slips, trips, and falls.

☐ Preventing lifting and material handling injuries.

☐ Handling emergencies and providing first aid.

☐ OSHA compliance.

In developing specific training sessions, make accommodations for employees' language differences, educational levels, and work experience. Keep each presentation simple, practical, and uniform, but cover topics in sufficient detail. You may want to require employees to sign a statement that they received safety training. Keep these statements in employees' personnel records. At the very least, retain complete records of the training sessions and the attendees.

Train employees to report to managers all accidents they are involved in or witness. The data gathered can help establishments better manage accidents that occur, prevent future accidents, and help the establishment comply with OSHA record-keeping requirements and, when applicable, workers' compensation claims.

An overall approach to training should integrate specific safety procedures into on-the-job training. As a manager, set an example for your employees. By following your own safety rules, you are also training your employees. Positively communicating safety is vital to a successful program. Stress safety's benefits. Emphasize that a safety program prevents accidents, suffering, and loss of income. A constructive program makes the establishment a better and more secure place to work and visit and helps limit the negative effects of accidents.

Emergency Training and Procedures

The wide and expanding range of crisis-related liabilities means that foodservice establishments must be prepared. Emergencies can include natural disasters, fires, explosions, violence, and other events that injure many people or cause great harm, damage, or serious misfortune. An effective safety program that includes training in emergency procedures can reduce your vulnerability to lawsuits and establish procedures and strategies for handling lawsuits and investigations that do occur.

A basic general emergency plan establishes the foundation to efficiently handle any situation. Establish a crisis management team. The team should have between five and eight members. Designate the key decision makers during an emergency and delegate their responsibilities. A team leader, a spokesperson, and a legal advisor also should be named.

Document emergency plans and communicate them to employees. Emergency plans should be simple and straightforward, as they will most likely be consulted in an actual emergency. The American Red Cross, police, or fire department might provide first aid training and can offer strategies for handling special situations. Keep emergency supplies on hand and make sure employees know where they are located.

Even after a crisis is over, it can affect customers and employees as well as the premises, cash flow, and profitability. The organization and effort put into planning for and managing a crisis should extend to several points:

- ☐ Document all incidents, including damages incurred.

- ☐ Analyze the sequence of events in the crisis. If applicable, try to discover the original cause.

- ☐ Assess the effectiveness of your emergency planning and response.

- ☐ Develop a communications plan to supply accurate information to employees, the public, the media, the police, and governmental agencies.

Emergency training should be a part of your regular safety training schedule. Well-prepared employees (and managers) are your best bet for surviving the crisis and getting back to business. Regular training can help give your employees the basic skills they need, but practice under pressure is also necessary. Drills and exercises can help you simulate crisis conditions.

References

1. Workplace Safety Program, which consists of the following five titles: *Designing and Implementing a Safety Program; Preventing Burns; Preventing Cuts; Preventing Lifting and Carrying Injuries;* and *Preventing Slips, Trips, and Falls* © 1999 The Educational Foundation of the National Restaurant Association

Learning Objectives

You will be asked to:

☆ Evaluate and document a security program for an establishment.

☆ State methods and procedures that may prevent internal and external theft in an establishment.

☆ Recognize the percentage of sales lost to theft.

☆ Select when managers should perform a general security audit.

☆ Recommend aspects of a security policy managers should introduce to employees.

☆ Determine the first step to take when a theft of customer property is reported.

Security

Just as with a safety program, before you develop a security program, conduct a general security audit to identify any areas that are or might be hazardous to employees and customers. The results will help you develop a security program that best meets your needs. The main areas to review in a general security audit are facilities, general security systems, cash management and banking procedures, employee work procedures, management work procedures, customer security, and security emergency procedures.

The audit findings will help identify any areas that are security risks. After completing the audit, develop security program guidelines using existing security directives and insurance carrier's requirements. Write a policy statement to outline intent and include a mission statement, a program overview, and a description of employee and manager duties. This helps you communicate your standards to your employees. Several topics to cover in your security policy are the definition of theft, drug and alcohol use and abuse on and off the premises, fighting or abusive behavior, and penalties for any policy violation.

Develop written descriptions of security procedures and standards for correct completion. Security measures should be covered in your employee training program. Areas to emphasize include:

☐ The damage that theft and carelessness cause for the establishment, co-workers, and the work environment.

☐ Management's determination to control security dangers while respecting employee privacy.

☐ The procedures for employees to follow for reporting employee theft or other crimes and security issues.

Facility Security

A well-designed facility helps deter theft and prevent personal violent crimes. Both the front and back of the house must be designed with security in mind. Storerooms near doors that lead to parking areas, as well as unsupervised or rarely inspected employee locker rooms, are ideal hiding places for potential interlopers and thieves. The area around cash registers should be lit well enough to be in plain sight of management or other employees. Dark corners or hidden booths are ideal hiding places for would-be thieves waiting for slow periods or closing time.

The outside premises must be included in security management as well. Poorly lit or isolated parking lots invite attacks on both employees and patrons. For safety, employees should be scheduled in pairs or groups, and a manager should always be a member of the opening and closing teams.

Preventing Theft

The National Restaurant Association has noted that approximately five cents of every dollar of sales is lost to theft, and that four cents of that is lost to employees. During employee orientation and training, define theft for your employees. Be very specific about your company's employee policies. Go over the policy with employees item by item.

Ordering and vendor source information should be available to authorized employees only. Before accepting shipments, they should be examined for correct quality and quantity. The authorized employee and delivery person should sign all invoices. All goods should be moved immediately to the proper storage area. A manager or employee should accompany delivery people at all times. All storage areas should be locked with controlled access. All stock should be logged into the inventory system as it is received with a date, inventory number and accurate count. All goods issued should be documented with a written receipt signed by the manager or other authorized person. The trash area should be monitored for stolen food, supplies, or equipment.

The back office and all management offices should be locked with limited access. Only a limited number of people should know combinations to safes. Only the manager and accounting employees should have access to the computer and cash register. Check financial records for money or product losses. Blank checks, deposit slips, gift certificates, and coupons should be locked in a safe. Deposits should be made daily. Reconcile bank statements regularly. Regularly inspect and audit inventories and separate financial duties. All inventory, cash handling, or bookkeeping should be checked by another person or a supervisor. Most experts recommend using sequentially numbered guest checks to control the flow of food from the kitchen and customer payments in return.

Customers or others may victimize other patrons by stealing their personal items, vandalizing, or stealing their vehicles in the establishment's parking lot. Despite the presence of signs warning customers that they are responsible for their vehicles, the courts may hold establishments responsible for customer cars and their contents in the parking lot.

Usually, the victims of theft report these crimes to the establishment. The establishment should immediately call the police. If a victim accuses another patron of personal theft, a manager should call the police, but proceed very cautiously. Caution both the victim and the accused against violence. Ideally, the victim and the accused will wait for
the police to arrive to begin an investigation. The establishment should restrain the accused only in self-defense or to protect others. Consult an attorney about the establishment's obligations in apprehending suspects.

Customers have a variety of tactics they use to avoid paying their bill. Theft of services includes credit card fraud, passing bad checks, passing counterfeit money, coupons, or gift certificates, and walking out unobserved. The cash register is a key point for coordinating security efforts against fraud. Credit card and bad check offender lists, as well as reference sources for checking driver's licenses, credit cards, checks, money, gift certificates, and coupons should be updated as necessary and kept near each cash register. Employees should be trained in correct procedures for identifying when customers try to avoid paying their bill.

Documenting an incident of theft should be conducted as soon as possible. Dismissing employees who steal should be documented and witnessed. Once theft is proven, document the entire event and the course of action that was taken.

References

1. *Presenting Service: The Ultimate Guide for the Foodservice Professional* by Lendal H. Kotschevar, FMP and Valentino Luciani ©1996 The Educational Foundation of the National Restaurant Association

2. *Legal Aspects of Hospitality Management, Second Edition* by John E.H. Sherry ©1994 The Educational Foundation of the National Restaurant Association

Review Questions

The following questions are structured to draw from your experience and education as much as this manual's content. Some questions may also prompt review of a topic listed in the references at the end of each section.

Food Safety

1. Which of the following describes the Uniform Commercial Code?

    A. A document listing unsafe food handling practices.

    B. A listing of potentially hazardous foods.

    C. A code outlining security measures for foodservice operations.

    D. A means by which a person can seek compensation for illness from contaminated food products.

2. A person shows up at a restaurant claiming to be a health inspector. What should the manager do?

    A. Ask to see identification.

    B. Ask to see an inspection warrant.

    C. Ask for a hearing to determine if the inspection is necessary.

    D. Ask for a twenty-four hour postponement to prepare for the inspection.

3. Which of the following agencies enforce food safety in a restaurant?

    A. The FDA

    B. The Centers for Disease Control (CDC)

    C. State or local health departments

    D. The USDA

4. Food codes developed by state agencies are

    A. minimum standards necessary to ensure food safety.

    B. maximum standards necessary to ensure food safety.

    C. voluntary guidelines for establishments to follow.

    D. inspection practices for grading meats and meat products.

5. Which of the following is a goal of the food-safety inspection process?

    A. To evaluate the sanitation and food-safety practices within the establishment

    B. To protect the public's health

    C. To convey new food-safety information to establishments

    D. All of the above

6. The health department inspector has reported that the restaurant next door to you has a major problem with cockroaches. She checks your kitchen and finds all of the following situations present. Which one would suggest that you might also have a cockroach problem?

    A. She sees that the screen on the service door needs to be repaired.

    B. She picks up a bit of sawdust from a corner of the dry storeroom.

    C. She sees black grains that look like pepper under the refrigerator.

    D. She finds no small holes burrowed into the storeroom.

7. The responsibility for the sanitary operation of an establishment rests with
   A. the state health department.
   B. the manager/operator.
   C. the health inspector.
   D. the FDA.

8. Violations noted on the inspection report should be
   A. discussed in detail with the inspector.
   B. corrected within forty-eight hours or less if they are critical.
   C. explored to determine why they occurred.
   D. all of the above.

9. An establishment can be closed for all of the following reasons except
   A. a significant lack of refrigeration in the establishment.
   B. a backup of sewage in the establishment.
   C. a serious infestation of insects or rodents in the establishment.
   D. a minor violation in the establishment that was not corrected within twenty-four hours.

10. Unsafe foodhandling procedures are prohibited by health codes and
    A. state laws.
    B. health services.
    C. the Better Business Bureau.
    D. restaurant associations.

11. The presence of harmful substances in food is called
    A. spoilage.
    B. contamination.
    C. *Salmonellosis.*
    D. foodborne illness.

12. If a food smells, tastes, or looks unacceptable it is considered
    A. toxic.
    B. contaminated.
    C. spoiled.
    D. unsanitary.

13. Bacteria grow and multiply most rapidly at temperatures between
    A. 0°F and 35°F (-8°C and 2°C).
    B. 20°F and 45°F (-7°C and 7°C).
    C. 41°F and 140°F (5°C and 60°C).
    D. 140°F and 190°F (60°C and 88°C).

14. Generally, disease-producing bacteria grow best when the environment is
    A. neutral or nearly neutral.
    B. highly alkaline.
    C. highly acidic.
    D. very dry.

15. Bacteria cannot grow, but most are not killed, in which kind of storage?
    A. Steam table
    B. Dry
    C. Refrigerator
    D. Freezer

16. Which of the following foods is most likely to harbor harmful bacteria?
    A. Chicken livers
    B. Raw onions
    C. White flour
    D. Lemon juice

17. Which of the following are potentially hazardous foods?

    A. Pasta

    B. Bananas and kiwifruit

    C. Broccoli and cauliflower

    D. Fish and tofu

18. Which type of food would be the most likely to cause a foodborne illness?

    A. Tomato juice

    B. Baked potatoes

    C. Stored whole wheat flour

    D. Dry powdered milk

19. Which of the following is *not* a basic characteristic of foodborne mold?

    A. It grows well in sweet acidic foods with low water activity.

    B. Freezing temperatures prevent or reduce its growth but do not destroy it.

    C. Its cells and spores may be killed by heating, but the toxins it produces may not be destroyed.

    D. It needs a host to survive.

20. Your restaurant is closed Sunday and Monday. Tuesday morning you open the restaurant and notice that the refrigerator is not running. When you check the internal thermometer, it reads 50°F (10°C). What should you do with the fresh ground beef in the refrigerator?

    A. Cook it and serve it within two hours.

    B. Freeze it right away.

    C. Discard it.

    D. Re-chill it immediately to below 41°F (5°C).

21. In refrigerated storage, it is proper to

    A. cool stocks and soups in their original pots.

    B. store foods on solid shelves.

    C. place raw foods above cooked foods.

    D. store dairy products separately from other foods.

22. Proper temperatures for dry storage areas are between

    A. 0°F and 25°F (-18°C and -4°C).

    B. 25°F and 50°F (-4°C and 10°C).

    C. 50°F and 75°F (10°C and 24°C).

    D. 75°F and 85°F (24°C and 29°C).

23. Your storeroom has a white line painted on the floor around the perimeter of the room. It extends six inches from the wall. What is the purpose of this line?

    A. It seals the floor against moisture seeping from the walls.

    B. It serves as a reminder to employees to keep stored items away from the walls.

    C. It works as a repellent against nesting mice.

    D. It works as a repellent against cockroaches.

24. Which step in food-preparation kills most disease-causing organisms?

    A. Freezing

    B. Thawing

    C. Slicing

    D. Cooking

25. Cross-contamination refers to

    A. the movement of bacteria from one food to another, or from work surfaces or equipment to food.

    B. soil or bacteria transferred from one kitchen department to another.

    C. employees infecting each other with bacteria.

    D. people getting bacteria from animals or animal products.

26. A failure to heat or cook food thoroughly is the most frequently cited factor in
    A. foodborne illness.
    B. customer dissatisfaction.
    C. the need for standardized recipes.
    D. the need for employee training manuals.

27. The best way to cool a stock pot of soup is to
    A. set it off the range top to cool for one hour and then refrigerate it.
    B. let it cool completely at room temperature and then refrigerate it.
    C. set the pot in ice water and stir to cool, then refrigerate it.
    D. place it in the refrigerator as soon as it finishes cooking.

28. The best reason for establishing a HACCP system is that it
    A. is required by the U.S. Food and Drug Administration (FDA).
    B. helps prevent foodborne illness.
    C. eliminates the risk of lawsuits.
    D. reduces the need for expensive equipment.

29. Identify the operational step not found in a usual HACCP flowchart.
    A. Receiving
    B. Reheating
    C. Cooling
    D. Compacting

30. In the HACCP system, a critical control point is a tool with which
    A. monitoring foodhandling steps becomes optional.
    B. hazards can be prevented, minimized, and eliminated.
    C. risk of foodborne illness is eliminated.
    D. certain high-risk foods can be eliminated from the menu.

31. You scoop some ice from your restaurant's ice storage bin and notice a drinking glass inside. The glass is missing a large piece of the rim. You find the chunk at the bottom of the storage bin. What should you do?
    A. Inspect each cube carefully by hand before serving the ice in beverages.
    B. Discard all of the ice and clean out the bin before restarting the icemaker.
    C. Transfer the ice to a clean container and flush out the bin before putting the ice back.
    D. No action is needed since you found both pieces of the glass.

32. Which serving method is most likely to protect the safety of the food being served?
    A. Using stainless-steel tongs to serve hot rolls directly to customers at the table
    B. Using a clean coffee cup to ladle soup into individual serving bowls
    C. Using a drinking glass to scoop ice cubes out of the icemaker storage compartment
    D. Using a teaspoon to scoop a serving of ice cream out of a five-gallon tub

33. Which of the following does not represent a potential food safety problem for a self-service lunch buffet?
    A. A bowl of macaroni salad that has been sitting on a table at room temperature from 11:00 a.m. to 3:30 p.m.
    B. A chafing dish of chicken a la king served at a temperature of 120°F (49°C)
    C. Vegetable soup served from a large bowl
    D. A platter of fresh vegetables presented directly on ice

34. Hash brown potatoes are a popular item on your hotel's breakfast buffet. They are served in a chafing dish that has its own heat source and an external dial thermometer. How can you ensure that the potatoes are safe to eat?

    A. Every two hours, measure the internal temperature of the potatoes with a thermometer.

    B. Every two hours, record the temperature reading on the chafing dish's external thermometer.

    C. Every hour, add fresh hot potatoes to the potatoes already in the chafing dish.

    D. Every hour, turn up the heat on the chafing dish to 165°F (74°C).

35. Which of the following is an appropriate service of an uncooked food?

    A. Raw fish in sushi, held for several hours and served at room temperature

    B. Unshucked oysters on ice, partitioned off from other ready-to-eat foods

    C. Raw chicken with fresh bread, served on a salad bar next to cut raw vegetables

    D. Raw lamb kibbe, served on an appetizer tray with cold stuffed grape leaves, relishes, salads and other ready-to-eat foods

36. Which of the following best describes the term "clean"?

    A. Free of disease-causing bacteria

    B. Inspected for the presence of rodents and pests

    C. Free of visible dirt

    D. Scraped and rinsed with warm water

37. When an official arrives to inspect a foodservice operation, the manager should

    A. accompany the official on the inspection.

    B. ask the official to inspect certain areas only.

    C. instruct employees to stop working.

    D. ask the official to return after the operation closes.

38. After you've washed your hands, which of the following items can you use to dry your hands?

    A. Your apron

    B. Single-use paper towels

    C. A common cloth towel

    D. A wiping cloth

39. Which of the following is the proper procedure for washing your hands?

    A. Run hot water, moisten hands and apply soap, rub hands together, apply sanitizer, dry hands.

    B. Run hot water, moisten hands and apply soap, rub hands together, rinse hands, dry hands.

    C. Run cold water, moisten hands and apply soap, rub hands together, rinse hands, dry hands.

    D. Run cold water, moisten hands and apply soap, rub hands together, rinse hands, apply sanitizer, dry hands.

40. Which hand-drying method is not recommended for use in a handwashing station?

    A. Forced-air dryer

    B. Single-use paper towels

    C. A common hand towel

    D. A continuous-cloth towel system

41. Hands should be washed after which of the following activities?

    A. Touching your hair

    B. Drinking

    C. Sneezing

    D. All of the above

42. Which of the following personal behaviors can contaminate food?

    A. Touching a pimple

    B. Touching hair

    C. Nose picking

    D. All of the above

43. Which of the following situations is most likely to protect the safety of food by minimizing human hand contact?

    A. A foodhandler uses metal tongs to place cooked beef onto a bun.

    B. A foodhandler sneezes into a tissue before handling food.

    C. A foodhandler uses hand lotion after washing her hands.

    D. A foodhandler drinks from a sanitary plastic cup while preparing food.

44. Becky has an unhealed sore on the back of one hand. Can Becky perform her regular foodhandling duties?

    A. Yes, if Becky's doctor provides a certificate that the sore is not contagious.

    B. Yes, if Becky agrees to use an antiseptic hand lotion between jobs.

    C. Yes, if the sore is bandaged and Becky wears a glove to protect the bandage.

    D. No, Becky should stay home from work until the sore has healed.

45. Kim wore disposable gloves while she formed raw ground beef into patties. When she was finished, she continued to wear the gloves while she sliced hamburger buns. What mistake did Kim make?

    A. She failed to change her gloves and wash her hands after handling raw meat and before handling a ready-to-eat food item.

    B. She failed to wash her hands before wearing the same gloves to slice the buns.

    C. She failed to wash and sanitize her gloves before handling the buns.

    D. She failed to wear reusable gloves.

46. Stephanie has a small cut on her finger and is about to prepare chicken salad. How should Stephanie's manager respond to the situation?

    A. Send Stephanie home immediately.

    B. Cover the hand with a glove or finger cot.

    C. Cover the cut with a clean, dry bandage, and a glove or finger cot.

    D. Cover the cut with a clean bandage.

47. Which of the following policies should be implemented at establishments?

    A. Employees must not smoke while preparing or serving food.

    B. Employees must not eat while in food-preparation areas.

    C. Employees must not chew gum or tobacco while preparing or serving food.

    D. All of the above.

48. Foodhandlers should be excluded from working with or around food if they are experiencing which of the following symptoms?

    A. Sneezing, itching, watery eyes

    B. Fever, vomiting, diarrhea

    C. Fatigue, headache, sweating

    D. Coughing, sore throat

49. Which item of personal apparel would most likely cause food to become unsafe?

    A. Earrings

    B. A dark-colored shirt

    C. A baseball-type cap

    D. A pair or athletic shoes

50. Management can play a key role in promoting personal hygiene by

    A. providing hand lotion in handwashing stations.

    B. providing reusable gloves for foodhandlers.

    C. modeling proper behavior at all times.

    D. permitting smoking in food-preparation areas.

51. A patron has telephoned a restaurant claiming that he contracted food poisoning from the chicken salad he ate there. The manager's most appropriate response is to

    A. tell the patron that it is impossible that the restaurant is as fault.

    B. apologize and offer to pay for all medical expenses.

    C. document the information and investigate.

    D. taste the leftover chicken salad to see whether anything is wrong with it.

52. In order for a foodborne illness to be considered an "outbreak," how many people must experience the illness after eating the same food?

    A. 1

    B. 2

    C. 10

    D. 20

53. Which is a proper container for garbage?

    A. A covered plastic bin

    B. An enclosed wire-mesh bin

    C. A stainless-steel storage container

    D. A ceramic tile-lined container

54. Where should kitchen trash containers be cleaned?

    A. In the "scrape" sink of a commercial three-compartment sink

    B. In a designated area away from food-preparation areas

    C. In a special area equipped with a bleach bath

    D. Any place in the kitchen where there is a floor drain

55. In order to reduce the volume of garbage and trash, foodservice operators can use grinders, pulpers, and

    A. composting.

    B. landfills.

    C. source reduction.

    D. mechanical compacting.

56. Which of the following practices reduces waste?

    A. Purchase pears individually wrapped in tray-pack containers

    B. Switch from buying milk in 5-gallon plastic containers to buying ½ gallon paper cartons

    C. Bake potatoes without wrapping them in aluminum foil

    D. Change from linen napkins to paper napkins in the dining room

57. Through a system of source reduction, foodservice operations are able to do which of the following?

    A. Decrease the bulk of their solid waste before recycling or disposing of it.

    B. Keep solid waste on the operation's property longer before disposal.

    C. Burn solid waste and garbage safely.

    D. Decrease the amount of disposable products used.

58. Which of the following is not a measure for controlling pests?

    A. Sealing the space around a pipe that exits the building

    B. Setting up a spring trap in the corner of the room

    C. Placing a chemical bait trap in the dishwashing area

    D. Setting out a multi-catch trap behind the icemaker machine

59. You have an outdoor dining area at your establishment. Which of the following practices do you want to avoid?

    A. Using lights that do not attract insects

    B. Using citronella candles

    C. Installing a "bug zapper" in a serving area

    D. Mowing the grass prior to opening the patio

Safety and Security

60. Which of the following organizations may conduct unannounced safety inspections?

    A. The Equal Employment Opportunity Commission

    B. The Occupational Safety and Health Administration

    C. The United States Department of Agriculture

    D. The National Restaurant Association

61. The Occupational Safety and Health Act requires foodservice operators to

    A. provide insurance for work-related accidents.

    B. take steps to reduce job hazards.

    C. guarantee workers that accidents will not occur.

    D. compensate employees for loss of pay due to accidents.

62. Which one of the following best describes a foodservice establishment's responsibility for complying with OSHA standards?

    A. A foodservice establishment is totally exempt and not required to report injuries or accidents to OSHA.

    B. Only foodservice establishments in certain areas are required to report work-related injuries and illnesses to OSHA.

    C. Foodservice employers must comply with all applicable safety and health standards.

    D. The Bureau of Labor Statistics demands that all establishments keep records of work-related injuries and illnesses.

63. When working with an OSHA inspector,

    A. record the inspector's comments during the visit.

    B. offer the inspector food or another item to make him or her more comfortable.

    C. you should not ask any questions until after the inspection.

    D. you may not discuss any alleged violations.

64. An employee handling an injured guest should

    A. notify the establishment's attorney before talking with the guest.

    B. record the event from the witnesses' and guests' perspectives.

    C. try to convince the guest that the accident is not the establishment's fault.

    D. offer medical advice.

65. Reasonable care is the
    A. anticipation that a particular action will likely result in harm or injury.
    B. standard of care expected from a medical professional.
    C. standard or degree of care, precaution, or diligence expected in a particular set of circumstances.
    D. person's awareness of conditions that could violate a legal requirement.

66. Which of the following is the best example of providing reasonable care?
    A. Posting a warning for known or foreseeable danger
    B. Carrying insurance coverage for excess liability
    C. Having all employees bonded
    D. Hiring security guards

67. Physical hazards can be
    A. toxic.
    B. corrosive.
    C. tissue-irritating.
    D. explosive.

68. The most commonly found chemicals in food services are cleaning products, pesticides, and
    A. cooking fuels.
    B. paint removers.
    C. paint thinners.
    D. weed killers.

69. OSHA's Hazard Communication Standard is also known as
    A. Right-to-Complain.
    B. Right-to-Know.
    C. Right-to-Communicate.
    D. Right-to-Conceal.

70. It is required by the OSHA Hazard Communication Standard to
    A. keep a written inventory of all chemicals used or stored in your establishment.
    B. display Poster No. 2203.
    C. distribute copies of the labels you will use on chemical containers.
    D. have MSDSs locked in the manager's office.

71. HAZCOM training should be
    A. an ongoing process that includes annual refresher meetings for all employees.
    B. forced upon employees.
    C. done only when OSHA visits your establishment.
    D. given only once a year.

72. Employees should receive chemicals in
    A. containers even if they are leaking.
    B. boxes even if they are not properly sealed.
    C. the manufacturer's original labeled containers.
    D. containers with smudged labels.

73. When handling hazardous chemicals
    A. be sure the work area is not ventilated.
    B. never mix chemicals unless instructions call for mixing.
    C. reuse as many chemical containers as you can.
    D. there is never a need to wear personal protective equipment.

74. When dispensing chemicals, employees should
    A. only use approved containers.
    B. spray near their eyes.
    C. always use more than they need.
    D. pour excess chemicals down the handwashing sink.

75. What does MSDS stand for?

    A. Material Security Data System

    B. Material Security Data Sheet

    C. Material Safety Data System

    D. Material Safety Data Sheet

76. Which of the following information is not required to be on an MSDS?

    A. Chemical name

    B. Hazardous components

    C. Expiration date

    D. Manufacturer's name

77. Which of the following should be the focus of written safety procedures?

    A. Penalties for not following the procedures

    B. What to do, how to do it, and standards for correct completion

    C. Rewards for following the procedures

    D. The individuals who will be supervising the procedures

78. When should an employee be trained in safety?

    A. As part of new employee orientation and when new equipment, menu items, and procedures are introduced

    B. After one year in a particular job

    C. After an accident occurs

    D. After he or she has been promoted to supervisor

79. Which of the following employee practices should a manager correct?

    A. Throwing away broken glass in an all-purpose garbage can

    B. Cutting vegetables with a sharp knife

    C. Using a tray to carry several drinks

    D. Using a step stool to reach a top shelf

80. Which of the following is true about evacuation routes?

    A. Routes should include elevators whenever possible.

    B. Routes should include areas where there are windows.

    C. Routes should provide every employee with one good exit.

    D. Routes should end outside and away from the building.

81. When should you fight a fire?

    A. If there is thick smoke

    B. If serious damage might occur to the building

    C. If the fire is less than three or four feet high and wide

    D. If you are strong enough to operate the extinguisher

82. First-aid training should include all of the following *except* how to

    A. aid choking victims.

    B. treat minor injuries.

    C. revive someone who has stopped breathing.

    D. administer medication.

83. In most cases, an incident report is

    A. submitted directly to the police.

    B. completed only in the event of a lawsuit.

    C. completed immediately following an occurrence.

    D. not usually necessary.

84. When should managers establish a crisis management team?

    A. As they begin to develop a crisis management plan

    B. Immediately following a crisis

    C. Every year

    D. After developing a crisis management plan, in order to implement it

85. Your crisis management team should include between five and eight staff members, a team leader, a spokesperson, and a

    A. firefighter.

    B. legal advisor.

    C. police officer.

    D. paramedic.

86. Which of the following is the most appropriate policy for an operation to take regarding handling media inquiries during or after a crisis?

    A. Employees should be encouraged to answer all questions truthfully.

    B. A designated manager should answer reporters' questions with facts.

    C. Managers should give no comments to reporters.

    D. Managers should talk only to reporters who agree to let the manager review the story before printing or airing.

87. When should managers perform a general security audit?

    A. Before developing a security program

    B. After a crime has taken place

    C. When planning a new facility

    D. When hiring security guards

88. Ideally, managers should introduce security measures to employees through

    A. the employee training program.

    B. discussion when accidents occur.

    C. discussion when an employee is caught stealing.

    D. on-site demonstrations by police officers.

89. To measure the success of your security program, you should

    A. develop an action plan for future improvements to the program.

    B. use orientation training to keep security awareness high.

    C. compare the costs of incidents to the costs of the program.

    D. conduct security audits on a frequent basis.

90. Which of the following is a closing procedure you should train your employees to follow?

    A. Make sure each employee leaves the establishment one at a time, so you can check their bags.

    B. Check the building to see that no one is hiding in closets, restrooms, storage areas, or offices.

    C. Lock cash, guest checks, register tapes, and other important documents in cash register drawers.

    D. Let only customers you personally know back into the establishment after the doors have been locked.

91. The greatest threat to internal security exists when an employee locker room area is located near a(n)

    A. exit.

    B. dining room.

    C. kitchen.

    D. manager's office.

92. If a manager decides to be lenient in the event of proven employee theft, the decision should be based on the
    - A. age of the employee only.
    - B. evidence surrounding the incident.
    - C. number of years worked only.
    - D. dollar value of the theft.

93. You should monitor employees on a daily basis by
    - A. inspecting employees' lockers.
    - B. inspecting all packages brought in and out.
    - C. noting any changes in employees behavior.
    - D. assigning one employee to guard the locker room door.

94. A guest has just told a server that someone took her purse from next to her chair. The first thing the server should do is
    - A. call the police.
    - B. question the suspected guest.
    - C. take a written statement from the accusing guest.
    - D. lock the operation's doors.

95. Which of the following actions should be taken if a fight is occurring in your establishment?
    - A. Call the police immediately.
    - B. Step in between the fighters.
    - C. Tell the fighters to move the fight outside.
    - D. Try to move the fighters to a quiet area of the restaurant.

96. A refusal to pay differs from an inability to pay in what way?
    - A. Refusals rarely happen.
    - B. Managers should only be concerned with refusals.
    - C. Refusal is a theft, whereas inability is often due to a customer's oversight.
    - D. Claiming inability is always an attempt to cheat the operation.

Answer Key

Food Safety

1. D	16. A	31. B	46. C
2. A	17. D	32. A	47. D
3. C	18. B	33. D	48. B
4. A	19. D	34. A	49. A
5. D	20. C	35. B	50. C
6. C	21. D	36. C	51. C
7. B	22. C	37. A	52. B
8. D	23. B	38. B	53. A
9. D	24. D	39. B	54. B
10. A	25. A	40. C	55. D
11. B	26. A	41. D	56. C
12. C	27. C	42. D	57. D
13. C	28. B	43. A	58. A
14. A	29. D	44. C	59. C
15. D	30. B	45. A	

Safety and Security

60. B	79. A
61. B	80. D
62. C	81. C
63. A	82. D
64. B	83. C
65. C	84. A
66. A	85. B
67. D	86. B
68. A	87. A
69. B	88. A
70. A	89. C
71. A	90. B
72. C	91. A
73. B	92. B
74. A	93. C
75. D	94. A
76. C	95. A
77. B	96. C
78. A	

Chapter 3 Outline

I. Recruiting and Hiring

    A. Staff Planning

    B. Recruiting Employees

    C. The Selection Process

    D. Legal Guidelines

    E. Hiring Employees

II. Orientation and Training

    A. Job Orientation

    B. Job Training

III. Shift Management and Scheduling Employees

    A. Shift Management

    B. Scheduling Employees

IV. Employee Supervision and Development

    A. Motivating Employees

        1. Building Teams

        2. Reducing Stress

        3. Delegating Responsibility

    B. Evaluating Performance

    C. The Disciplinary Process

    D. Exit Interviews

V. Sexual Harassment and Managing Diversity

    A. Sexual Harassment

    B. Managing Diversity

VI. Leadership and Communication Skills

    A. Leadership Skills

        1. Organizational Planning

        2. Decision Making

        3. Managing Time

    B. Communication Skills

        1. Meaningful Meetings

VII. Review Questions

Chapter 3
Human Resources Management

Learning Objectives

You will be asked to:

☆ Identify what document lists the tasks and responsibilities required of employees in filling a position.

☆ Specify the use of a job analysis.

☆ Outline the appropriate steps for calculating the number of additional servers required in an expansion.

☆ Determine where you should look first when filling a position above the entry level.

☆ Specify a job requirement that is permissible under the equal employment opportunity laws.

☆ Choose the primary reason to call a job candidate's reference.

☆ Given a help wanted advertisement, select that portion of the ad that shows evidence of possible discrimination.

☆ Determine a circumstance when questions about height, weight, and marital status might be included on an employment application.

The art and science of management consists of getting the job done through other people. Human resources management addresses many of the vital personnel issues that a manager confronts in the course of running an effective foodservice operation. The basic functions of recruiting, hiring, orienting, training, and supervising employees are fundamental to labor-intensive, service-oriented industry. Furthermore, employee development, motivation, team-building, and effective leadership cultivate good employees and employee relationships. Finally, a manager's strong leadership skills and effective communication are essential to a positive and productive work environment.

Recruiting and Hiring

Foodservice managers must constantly assess their human resources needs and fill positions with the most promising applicants. Hiring the right people is crucial to helping an operation accomplish its service and financial goals. To be most effective, managers should always be on the lookout for potential employees.

Staff Planning

The framework for identifying an operation's labor needs can be completed efficiently through planning. No work in an operation can be completed successfully until the staffing needs or tasks have been identified and translated into behavioral objectives. These objectives become the basis of a job analysis and determine the job categories that are necessary to accomplish the work within an organization.

For example, a job analysis might identify a server's task as "Serves guests." To become a behavioral objective, this task must be expanded in three ways. First, the objective must state clearly the task to be performed. Second, it must specify how the task is to be carried out. Third, the standard against which

the task will be measured must be stated clearly.
Applying these criteria, the task "Serves guests"
becomes a definite, unambiguous objective: "Serves
all food and beverages to guests at tables within
standards using correct table service techniques
as described in the (operation's) Table Service
Handbook." Behavioral objectives must include
directly measurable, observable actions, such as
serves, maintains, counts, demonstrates knowledge,
totals, and *prepares.* Unobservable standards, such as
understands, knows, and *seems,* communicate vague
and ambiguous expectations to employees.

Once clear behavioral objectives have been written,
they are compiled in each employee position's
job description. *(See Exhibit 3.1.)* Well-written
job descriptions serve managers in a number of
significant ways by doing the following:

- Describing an operation's labor needs.

- Delineating the skills required of employees
  filling each position.

- Outlining the areas in which employees
  must be trained.

Setting the standards by which employees'
performance will be measured and evaluated is the
purpose of the job description. Job descriptions can
protect an operation by ensuring clear and measurable
standards are communicated to employees.

Because they play such a vital role in human
resources management, writing clear job descriptions
must be a high priority for all foodservice managers.

Recruiting Employees

Recruiting qualified employees has always been a
concern of the foodservice industry, and it promises
to become an even more important issue in coming
years. The number of workers available, especially
the young workers who traditionally have made up
much of the foodservice workforce, are decreasing.
Managers will have to use their ingenuity to attract
the employees they need.

Internal sources for locating qualified job applicants
include employee recommendations (sometimes

---

1. Meets at the start of each shift with the chef to determine daily production needs.

2. Sets priorities to determine the order in which menu items will be prepared.

3. Prepares menu items according to methods described in the Standard Recipes Manual in enough time to ensure safe foodhandling and timely availability as described in the Kitchen Procedures Manual.

4. Informs the chef of inventory supply needs daily and as needs arise.

5. Maintains clean and sanitary conditions at all times as specified in the Sanitation Checklist.

6. Completes work as assigned by the chef.

7. Cleans and inspects work area at the end of each shift as specified in the Sanitation Checklist.

Exhibit 3.1
Job Description for Prep Cook

---

backed by bonuses for employees who refer
applicants) and the pool of former employees, such
as those returning to work after the birth of a child.
Current employees are the first pool from which to
screen applicants for positions above the entry level.

External sources include newspaper advertisements
and public and private employment agencies.
Newspaper ads pull in large numbers of applicants,
but managers must spend a considerable amount
of time reviewing applications and interviewing. A
good way to minimize the number of unqualified
applicants is to specify in the ad what experience or
skills are needed as well as a time to come in and
apply. This will attract only the candidates who
are interested enough in the job to set aside the
time to come in. Managers must remember to give
courteous attention to all applicants—each is part
of the restaurant's potential guest market.

Employment agencies refer more selectively, but
their fee structure usually limits managers to using
them only for filling high-level positions. In most

areas, state and other public employment services, such as community service groups and junior college placement services, are good sources of entry-level job applicants.

The Selection Process

It is obvious that poor selection methods are a major influence in high employee turnover in the hospitality industry. Selection methods should be developed with care. Proper tools, such as employment application forms, interviewing procedures, reference checks, and even pre-employment testing of assessments are important. Each screening tool should capture only information pertinent to a particular job; otherwise, you may violate legal requirements. These tools will assist you in predicting the behavior and performance of each job applicant.

It is important that qualified, experienced, and trained individuals administer these tools. Interviewers must understand the job position, the establishment, and how to solicit as much information as possible from the job applicant. Job applications can enhance the selection process, and often reveal more than an applicant intends. Incomplete answers, failure to answer all questions, or inaccurate responses to factual questions might indicate a resistance to following instructions. Poor writing skills might exclude an applicant from some jobs; writing competence may suggest that an applicant could take on a higher level of responsibility.

Interviews should focus on information about the applicant, organization, and position. Interviewers should try to determine some of the applicant's attitudes about the job and how well the job seems to fit in with the applicant's career plan. Hiring the right people cannot be overemphasized. In an industry that depends largely on personal service to guests, employees with whom the guest comes into contact must embody an operation's attitude, ethics, and image.

Legal Guidelines

A common, potentially illegal mistake managers make is not knowing the right questions to ask a prospective employee. The employment selection process is regulated by legal guidelines, which protect the civil rights of job applicants. Equal Employment Opportunity (EEO) is the legal right of all individuals to be considered for employment and promotion solely on the basis of their ability, merit and potential. EEO is mandated by law (The Civil Rights Act of 1964, The Age Discrimination Act of 1967, and Americans with Disabilities Act of 1991) and prohibits the intentional or unintentional discrimination of potential employees because of age, religion, sex, race, color, or mental or physical disability, national origin, or veteran status. Discrimination means that an employee is treated unfairly because of one or more of the previous conditions. Ability, merit, and potential are the basis of employee selection and advancement.

The Immigration Reform and Control Act (IRCA) of 1986 outlawed discrimination against legal immigrants to the United States. Employers may not ask applicants where they were born, nor require them to be U.S. citizens or even show a passport as identification. Proof of eligibility to work in the United States is all that is required of all employees, and someone with permanent work authorization cannot be favored over someone with temporary status. Because fines and even imprisonment of employers have increased in recent years, be aware of the law, and keep all screening practices job-related.

The processing of applications, conducting the job interview, checking references, and the administration of any pre-employment tests which result in employment must be based on job-related criteria. If they are not, they might be considered discriminatory. The best way to avoid potentially illegal, discriminatory, or offensive hiring practices is to keep all job requirements and application or interview questions directly related to the position. *(See Exhibit 3.2.)*

Questions should never be asked in the areas of age, race, marital status, national origin, religion, physical or mental disabilities, sex, transportation, children, height or weight, type of discharge from the military, credit history or references, or arrest record. You may ask if candidates have any handicaps that would prevent them from doing the job. After you have decided to present a job offer, the Immigration Reform and Control Act requires

---

Job requirement

Late hours

Remote location

Long-term commitment

Travel

Strenuous physical labor

Standing or walking for long shifts

Pleasant appearance

Discriminatory inquiry/requirement

Do you have children you need to be with at night?

Do you own a car?

Are you planning to have children?

Are you married?

Must be male.

Are you handicapped?

How much do you weigh?

Legal, job-related inquiry/requirements

This job entails late hours. Do you have any conflicts?

Do you have reliable transportation to work?

Can we count on your employment here for more than one or two years?

This job requires quite a bit of travel. Will that be a problem?

Must be able to lift 40-pound boxes and heavy machine parts.

Will you be comfortable standing/walking for long shifts?

Must maintain neat, well-groomed appearance.

Exhibit 3.2
Guidelines for Appropriate Job Recruiting

---

that you inquire about authorization to work in the United States and properly complete a Form I-9, and if the job candidate is an alien, you may request an Alien Registration Number.

While it is impossible to remove all of the risk from the hiring process, you can eliminate some by approaching employee selection systematically. Some type of candidate comparison form that lists candidates' work experience, strengths and weaknesses, and responses to interview questions can help do this.

Hiring Employees

If the applicant qualifies for the job vacancy and meets your interview criteria, a reference check should be made for all the positions listed on the job application before an offer is extended. While reference checks may not be a precise indicator of an employee's performance, they do provide an evaluation of the applicant's attributes and qualifications. A reference check should verify prior dates of employment and position.

If the job analysis, recruitment, and selection processes have been successful, the candidate can be offered the position. Once you have made your decision, contact the prospective employee immediately so you do not lose him or her to another employer. You will most likely make the offer by telephone, reiterating wages or salary, and ask whether the person needs time to consider your offer.

After a candidate has accepted your offer, send or give your new employee a formal letter outlining the terms of the offer, including position, wages or salary, starting date, work schedule, and any other pertinent information. After a candidate is hired, it is necessary to complete the I-9 (Employment Eligibility Verification Form), W-4 (Federal Withholding Form), and other local tax forms and paperwork necessary for maintaining a personnel file.

References

1. *Human Resources Management for the Hospitality Industry* by Mary L. Tanke, FMP ©1990 Delmar Publishers

2. *Supervision in the Hospitality Industry, Third Edition* by Jack E. Miller, FMP, Mary Porter, and Karen Eich Drummond, FMP ©1998 John Wiley and Sons, Inc.

Learning Objectives

You will be asked to:

☆ Select the primary goal of a new employee orientation program.

☆ Choose an appropriate subject for discussion during employee orientation.

☆ Recommend the most effective way to present organizational policies to new employees.

☆ Outline essential elements of all employee training.

☆ Explain the reason why a head server should be asked to help train new servers.

☆ Identify whether a training procedure is complete or lacking essential elements.

☆ Select an instructor most likely to turn out competent workers.

Orientation and Training

Effective orientation and training programs most often translate into lower employee turnover, lower costs, and higher profits. Orientation is the process of acquainting new employees with the organization's facility, present employees, and policies and procedures. Usually, the type and size of the organization dictates the form of orientation. For example, large chain operations might use audio-visual presentations, lectures, and printed handouts, while smaller operations may provide a typed manual, an individual tour, and introductions led by the supervisor.

Job Orientation

In any operation, managers can ensure that all employees get the same orientation by following an employee orientation checklist. A checklist helps organize what new workers should know and gives employees the information they need to acclimate themselves to the operation. The checklist should cover general topics such as:

☐ The goal of the introductory meeting.

☐ The history of the establishment.

☐ Key company goals related to the new employee's job.

☐ Organizational structure.

☐ Payroll policies.

☐ Work schedules.

☐ Safety measures and regulations.

☐ Compensation, benefits, and employee services.

One way to formalize procedures, avoid employee confusion, and enforce company policies is to prepare an employee manual. In addition to receiving job-related training such as a position manual, each new employee should receive a copy of an employee manual. Employers should keep a written, signed record of its receipt. The manual might be as simple as several typed pages stapled together, but it should cover the following key areas:

- Organization.
- Introduction to the establishment (including its history and goals).
- Pay policies.
- Work schedules and holidays.
- Appearance and uniforms.
- Break times and tip reporting.
- Sanitation and safety rules.
- Security and breakage.
- Employee reviews.
- Promotion policies, termination, and reasons for dismissal.
- Fringe benefits.
- Training procedures.

Preparing a manual will require examining policies for consistency and eliminating those that are of questionable value. In case of conflict or legal problems with employees, the employee manual might offer support. Be aware that an employee manual should enhance, not replace a new employee orientation program.

Job Training

After introducing an employee to the organization and other employees, job training begins. To offer the best training, be aware of the principles that guide the trainer/employee relationship. First, the learner and the trainer must be motivated. Most new workers will view training as a way to become independent and secure in their jobs. Workers already on the job may need more convincing about the value of training, but will likely be motivated by the chance to move up in the organization and trade their routine tasks for new ones.

Second, training should be individualized to the worker and the task. All trainees do not learn at the same rate, and learning might taper for a short time. Although the supervisor should always be sure employees are not bored or overtired, enthusiasm will level off and this is quite normal. Remember to keep the trainee involved in the training. Use hands-on experience and demonstrations as much as possible. Maintain two-way communication to encourage questions and comments. Set goals so the trainer and trainee always know where the session is going and what is to be accomplished. Finally, providing trainees with feedback and reinforcement is critical to their learning retention and motivation. Always emphasize positive results even when correcting wrong behaviors.

Training is unquestionably one of the surest ways to fill your operation with competent, motivated, and satisfied workers. Investing time and money in a training program—and in your employees—will translate into better performance, lower employee turnover, and satisfied customers.

References

1. *Human Resources Management for the Hospitality Industry* by Mary L. Tanke, FMP ©1990 Delmar Publishers

2. *Supervision in the Hospitality Industry, Third Edition* by Jack E. Miller, FMP, Mary Porter, and Karen Eich Drummond, FMP ©1998 John Wiley and Sons, Inc.

Shift Management and Scheduling Employees

Opening and closing the operation, shift transition, and the thoughtful scheduling of employees are essential skills for a manager to learn and apply.

Shift Management

Shift management encompasses an operation's timely and successful start-up, smooth transition between shifts, and a secure close-down. Opening the operation for the day includes an adherence to standardized start-up procedures, including a pre-opening review of the facilities to check for irregularities. A checklist can accomplish standard procedures and should deal with such items as cash and register management, cleanup and sanitation, maintenance procedures, and the security of the facility and its contents.

A smooth transition between employee shifts is necessary to achieve a consistently high level of service. Employee preparation for the shift or peak meal activity is essential in a smooth running operation. A premeal or preshift meeting can serve this purpose, particularly when operating volumes are high and staffing is low. Shift supervisors need to communicate with one another on a face-to-face and written basis. An operation log that records incidents and status reports is a valuable communication tool for an operation. It is also a valuable management and analytical tool for spotting patterns in an operation.

Finally, the close-down of an operation should be subject to a strict standardized procedure. As with the start-up, the operation should be inspected and secured at close-down.

Scheduling Employees

An important corollary task to shift management is the scheduling of employees.

An effective work schedule can ensure the correct number of employees at work at a given time. Schedules can be prepared weekly, monthly, or on a permanent basis. But shorter schedules allow for more flexibility, an important factor in unpredictable foodservice operations.

Managers should organize the employee work schedule with the aid of a *staffing guide,* which outlines basic personnel needs for a given period of time. To prepare a guide, determine the operation's service hours and the number of employees, by position, needed for each hour of service. Then, make a separate schedule for each job position.

Variable-cost (hourly) employees should be scheduled according to business volume. To determine the amount of *fixed-cost* (salaried) employees, the manager should study the positions that affect every job. During slower periods, the number of employees scheduled can be reduced. Using relief or part-time employees provides more flexibility and can help reduce labor costs.

After completing a schedule, post it so that all employees are aware of their hours. This posting should be made far enough in advance for employees to make plans to accommodate the schedule.

References

1. *Presenting Service: The Ultimate Guide for the Foodservice Professional* by Lendal H. Kotschevar, FMP and Valentino Luciani ©1996 The Educational Foundation of the National Restaurant Association

Learning Objectives

You will be asked to:

☆ Describe a common mistake supervisors make in an evaluation interview.

☆ Recommend a course of action in a situation when a long-term employee's performance suddenly slips.

☆ Outline the core elements of a program designed to retain good employees.

☆ Identify when workforce team spirit grows best.

☆ Explain what a manager must do when delegating responsibility to an employee.

☆ Given several examples, select the best example of delegating responsibility.

☆ State an action essential to effective discipline.

☆ Specify what a manager should do first before firing an employee.

☆ Describe how a manager should approach an employee in a potential discipline situation.

☆ State the key reasons why a manager should conduct an exit interview with all departing employees.

Employee Supervision and Development

Motivating Employees

The ideal manager motivates employees to become self-assured and independent in their jobs. In addition, managers should strive to encourage employees to form a cooperative, cohesive group that works toward common operational goals.

To get the most productivity from employees, managers must be motivated themselves. The motivated manager can channel energy toward helping workers fulfill their work goals and become a part of the work team. Let workers know when they are hired that their success depends on more than just washing dishes or delivering meals. Each employee's role in an organization is crucial to offering the best possible products and service to satisfied customers. Employees must know that they make the difference.

Bonuses can be given for the number of customers served or for using customers' names, but a costly incentive program is not the only way to motivate employees to perform well. Verbal praise for good work goes a long way toward developing a pride that translates into greater productivity. Well-placed positive reinforcement encourages more of the praised behavior.

Many people view the ability to grow within a company as an incentive. Growth can be in the form of training or a promotion and new title with added responsibility. Ongoing training provides the opportunity for staff input on such subjects as menu additions and augmented service. High employee morale depends largely on how much employees believe their employer respects their opinions and promotes from within. A clearly stated organizational vision also contributes greatly to employees' sense of pride and motivation.

Other simple morale boosters are staff parties, organized intramural sports, comfortable employee locker rooms, and advanced posting of schedules.

For seasonal workers in particular, organize functions that will bring them together to build identification with the establishment for their short stay. Formal incentives should tell employees that managers appreciate them as individuals and want them to stay.

Building Teams

Implementing work teams and fostering teamwork through training translates into higher productivity and profits, as well as more fulfilled managers and employees. Teamwork can be advantageous to an establishment in that it increases production, establishes an effective rewards system, defines of specific roles and tasks, and frees the manager to devote more time to managerial responsibilities.

The overwhelming majority of businesses that adopt a teamwork approach to organizing work experience a jump in productivity. Employees trained in team processes can accomplish more together than they could working alone as individuals. This is due to team members sharing knowledge and skills, picking up slack for each other when needed, building on each other's ideas, and encouraging each other. Productivity in a given work area is not limited to the abilities available among those regularly assigned to that area. People with needed skills can be brought onto the work team from other areas or departments.

Role and task definition are important parts of teamwork. Studies show that a worker's knowledge of his or her job and how it fits into the overall organization is often more important than pay level. In well-trained teams, employees are committed to team and organizational goals. They understand the overall operation, the role they play in it, and the functions and needs of other parts of the organization. This awareness of the larger picture helps keep down tensions between departments, work areas, and shifts because workers realize they are interdependent. Developing effective teams may also limit employee absenteeism and turnover. Employees also gain a sense of belonging.

An important factor in job satisfaction and employee morale is a reward system that employees perceive as fair. A teamwork setup can help a manager construct such a system when wages or salaries and other rewards are tied to group performance. Employees are more likely to feel they have a fair chance at rewards when they have support in achieving their goals.

Managers in organizations using self-directed teams are able to spend less time and energy in routine tasks, and more time managing. Because everyone works as a team, problems are caught sooner, so managers spend less time resolving crises. They have more time to spend on managerial tasks such as planning and employee development.

Reducing Stress

Building a motivated staff involves reducing group and individual stress. Although some stress spurs creativity and productivity, most stress results in strained relationships. Because of its negative impact on individuals and organizations, stress both on employees and managers has become an important supervisory issue in the foodservice industry.

As a concerned manager, it helps to recognize early warning signs of stress in your employees and yourself before job burnout—the inability to handle job stress that can result in frustration and reduce efficiency—occurs. Many physical, psychological, and performance symptoms can indicate stress. Physical changes, such as continual fatigue or weight changes, signal the body's reaction to a stressful event or ongoing stress. Psychological symptoms are usually more subtle. Stress can interfere with thought processes or cause depression, irrational actions or feelings, and irritability. Stress can transform the high achiever into someone who makes poor, erratic judgments, fails to meet deadlines, or even fails to come to work.

Poor time management is a significant source of stress. Poor management of one's time can make a person's workload feel overwhelming. It can make daily activities seem haphazard and without purpose. People who manage their time poorly often have trouble organizing and prioritizing work. A manager can help employees regain control over their time at work by showing them how they can make the best use of their time in accomplishing their daily tasks.

All stressors cannot and should not be eliminated from a person's life. A certain amount of stress enables a person to achieve an optimum level of performance. However, a healthier outlook and more effective coping techniques help minimize stress.

Delegating Responsibility

One way to work more efficiently, reduce stress, and motivate employees to excel is to delegate responsibility. Before any operation can be set in motion, top management must arrange a hierarchy of authority and responsibility to oversee implementation of all work assignments. By delegating responsibilities and clearly communicating the chain of command to all, the hierarchy will function properly and you will have more time to plan both for the unexpected and the future.

Delegation of responsibility differs from the assignment of tasks in two ways. First, it involves giving the employee accountability. Second, the responsibility delegated should be one that was done previously by the manager or supervisor. In other words, a manager *delegates* the responsibility of planning daily lunch specials to a head cook, but *assigns* the task of cleaning the floor of the walk-in refrigerator to a dishwasher.

When delegating responsibility, managers need to examine what is to be done and recognize the talents of the employees who can best carry them out. Delegating effectively means clearly communicating what someone is to do, what results are anticipated, and when these results are expected. Managers must follow through and hold each employee accountable for their work while still giving them the opportunity to handle the job in their own way. This does not mean that managers abdicate responsibility. They are still

accountable for the work of their staff. Above all, employees must have the authority and resources to get the job done. Nothing frustrates people more than being given responsibilities without the resources to carry them out.

Evaluating Performance

After employees are recruited, hired, oriented, trained, and are independently carrying out their job functions, their performance must be evaluated. The best way to measure employees' improvement is to institute a performance evaluation program. Formal evaluations give the manager and employee an opportunity to communicate and set performance goals. In addition, written evaluation forms help managers identify employees for promotion and raise low performance levels.

A good evaluation program begins the first day on the job and offers periodic review throughout an employee's history with a company. Evaluations should be performed regularly and as frequently as possible. To set the tone for productive evaluations, a copy of the evaluation form should be given to new employees as part of their general orientation. Managers should keep files on each employee and record any pertinent information, such as raises, special projects, extraordinary performance, problems with co-workers, and excessive tardiness. Written records are a way of remembering facts—both positive and negative—and of supporting any future decisions.

A common mistake managers make during evaluation is focusing on an employee's mistakes. From the beginning, employees should know that they will be evaluated based on the responsibilities stated in their job descriptions. All employees' ratings should increase with time and experience on the job. If employees are not performing well, the manager and employee must set goals to change the situation. This way, performance evaluations can be a very useful tool in improving employees' performance and making their relationship with the organization a more positive one. On the other hand, if performance does not improve, the manager must know when it is time to terminate the employee before bigger problems arise. All performance evaluations should be held in a private area, and results should be kept confidential between the employer and employee.

The Disciplinary Process

Every company should have a discipline policy that considers the workers' legal rights, any existing union contract, and, above all, a person's dignity. A fair and equitable disciplinary program includes standards for acceptable employee conduct. It also fosters individual and company goals while protecting the employee from unfair treatment. Once uniform work standards are set, the manager must communicate these rules to all employees.

Studies show that more rules are broken out of ignorance than out of willful wrongdoing. Unless employees know and understand regulations and the consequences of noncompliance, they cannot be expected to adhere to them. Determining the cause of a disciplinary problem may not change what happened, but it helps managers decide what action to take. It may be that discipline is not called for, but retraining may be necessary. There is a big difference between the cook who intentionally jams the food processor and one who lacks the training to operate the machine correctly. An effective discipline program educates, trains, and motivates workers to comply with reasonable demands.

In all aspects of employee supervision, managers must document occurrences of unacceptable employee behavior, since it is the pattern of repeated behavior, rather than one instance, that generally leads to disciplinary action and termination. In addition, employees must be made aware of all rules and procedures. When an infraction occurs, the manager should issue a verbal warning to the employee. A repeated offense warrants a written warning, and continued unacceptable behavior justifies termination if incidents have been properly documented.

Another important element of a disciplinary program is an assessment mechanism. The manager is usually expected to prove any wrongdoing and the need for discipline, and employees have the right to defend themselves. Rule violations should be dealt with when they are discovered. Part of any disciplinary process should be an opportunity to either modify the undesirable behavior or appeal the discipline.

To better understand how to handle discipline, consider the following three categories of employee problems.

1. **Rule-breaking and illegal acts.** Rules covering worker health and safety must always be followed, and infringements must be handled swiftly. Illegal acts, such as selling drugs at work or stealing, are cause for immediate termination. Rule infractions, such as abusive language and horseplay, may or may not receive action, depending upon the intent of the worker. A manager should seek action if foul language ridicules or degrades anyone's position. Horseplay that interferes with the flow of work or could cause injury must be stopped immediately, but clowning around that is part of social interaction is not necessarily bad. Fights among co-workers should always be prohibited. How to handle them depends upon the employees' work record and length of employment, the number of incidents by the individuals, whether there was injury, whether the safety or morale of other employees was affected, and the intent of those involved.

2. **Unsatisfactory performance.** Employees work slowly or make mistakes for many reasons. Some employees lack appropriate skills and capabilities to perform their job. These people need training, stronger supervision, or a move to a different position. Others lack the motivation to work. In this case, positive rewards for high quality and productivity—or an overall incentive program— might help. However, if you have instituted such programs and discussed alternative

behaviors with these employees without any changes, you may have to consider termination.

3. **Personal problems.** Employees' personal problems often are brought to work, and they can affect productivity and accuracy. The best action for managers to take in such situations is to talk with employees about performance issues and listen actively. Sometimes, just talking about problems relieves the tension enough for the employee to function better on the job. If the problem continues to affect work, direct the employee to a trained counselor, employee assistance program, or other resource. Every effort should be made to steer the employee toward the appropriate assistance. Above all, discussions between the manager and employee should be confidential, well documented, and focus on job-related performance issues.

Exit Interviews

When an employee leaves an establishment, whether it is voluntary or involuntary, a manager should have a meeting with the employee to discuss such issues as paycheck, benefits, rehiring privileges, and unemployment compensation. An exit interview can provide an organization with information regarding attrition in cases where management terminates and employee, but it can also provide useful information that may reveal weaknesses in the operation's work environment. The information provided in an exit interview may:

☐ Uncover weak human resources practices.

☐ Indicate a noncompetitive compensation plan.

☐ Locate specific sources of job dissatisfaction.

☐ Identify supervisors who do not follow the policies and procedures of the establishment.

Exit interviews can reveal the reasons why employees may not be happy at the establishment. With this information, a manager may change policies or procedures to promote job satisfaction and consequently reduce the rate of employee turnover. However, the information is only as good as the employee is honest. Not all employees feel comfortable in providing honest answers.

While an exit interview checklist may be helpful, the questions and content of an exit interview should be tailored to each particular situation. In voluntary termination cases, asking the employee what could be done to get the employee to stay may be a productive question than asking why the employee is leaving. Exit interviews should not be conducted on the employee's last day of employment, as that can be a day full of distractions for the employee.

References

1. *Human Resources Management for the Hospitality Industry* by Mary L. Tanke, FMP ©1990 Delmar Publishers.

2. *Supervision in the Hospitality Industry, Third Edition* by Jack E. Miller, FMP, Mary Porter, and Karen Eich Drummond, FMP ©1998 John Wiley and Sons, Inc.

Learning Objectives

You will be asked to:

☆ Give an example of a sexual harassment situation as well as an appropriate solution.

☆ Determine whether a sexual harassment situation exists and, if so, what type.

☆ Explain stereotyping.

☆ Identify the most significant obstacle that impedes employee advancement.

☆ Describe the legal statutes that prohibit sexual harassment and ethnic discrimination in the work place.

Sexual Harassment and Managing Diversity

Sexual Harassment

Sexual harassment of employees is against the law, and employers are wise to implement clear company policy guidelines on this issue. Operators who do not take steps to prevent harassment may indeed foster it and the accompanying legal problems. Employers can be held liable for harassment issued by both employees and customers. Supervising customers is more difficult than supervising employees, but on occasion it must be done, and sexual harassment of all employees—male and female—must be strictly prohibited and punished.

The Equal Employment Opportunity Commission's (EEOC) Guidelines on Sexual Harassment in the Workplace, issued in 1980, define sexual harassment as follows.

Unwelcome sexual advances, requests for sexual factors, and other verbal or physical conduct of a sexual nature constitute sexual harassment when (1) submission to such conduct is made either explicitly or implicitly a term or condition of an individual's employment, (2) submission to or rejection of such conduct by an individual is used as the basis for employment decisions affecting such individual, or (3) such conduct has the purpose or effect of unreasonably interfering with an individual's work performance or creating an intimidating, hostile, or offensive working environment.

Two elements are necessary to make a harassment determination: the conduct must be sexual and it must be unwelcome. To be considered sexual, the behavior:

☐ Must be sexual in nature but does not have to involve sexual relations or requests for such.

☐ May be physical, verbal, or visual.

☐ May occur inside or outside the workplace.

☐ Need not be directed at the complainant.

Even voluntary behavior may be unwelcome, as long as the victim did not solicit it or incite it.

According to the EEOC guidelines, an employer is responsible for sexually harassing acts of its employees regardless of whether the harassment was authorized or forbidden by the employer and regardless of whether the employer knew or should have known of its occurrence. An employer is also responsible for sexually harassing acts that occur between fellow employees when the employer or supervisory employees know or should have known of the harassment, unless the employer can show that it took immediate and appropriate corrective action. Finally, an employer is liable for sexually harassing acts of its non-employees when the employer knows or should have known of the harassment and fails to take immediate and appropriate corrective action.

Employers may also be held liable for a qualified employee's lost job opportunities when the supervisor has given a specific position or benefit to another employee who has submitted to their advances or with whom they have been romantically involved.

The courts recognize two types of sexual harassment, *quid pro quo* and *hostile environment.* Quid pro quo—"something for something"—is harassment in which submitting to a supervisor's sexual advances becomes necessary for getting or keeping a job. An employee's job security or advancement opportunities are linked to his or her acceptance of the supervisor's sexual advances. In hostile environment cases, an employee's psychological and emotional well being and working environment are significantly impeded by "unwelcome sexual advances or verbal or physical conduct of a sexual nature" initiated or ignored by a supervisor but without direct impact to an employee's job.

In addition to defining sexual harassment, the EEOC guidelines also direct employers to prevent sexual harassment by writing, communicating, and enforcing a sexual harassment policy which defines sexual harassment and provides for a designated investigator and complaint-resolution procedures.

Managing Diversity

Today's diverse workforce presents new challenges to the foodservice manager. Studies indicate the biggest barrier to employee advancement is workplace prejudice. Smart managers will realize it is poor business practice to waste any human resources potential, and that their operation's success depends on developing new attitudes toward nontraditional workers.

The first step to eliminating stereotypes in an organization is to become aware of one's prejudices and stereotypes. The second step is to learn about cultures represented in an organization. This provides information that can contradict and dissolve solidified stereotypes.

A manager's attitudes and behavior have a significant influence on how employees behave. A manager who sets a good example in a culturally diverse work place is honest with all employees about their performance; is available to all employees when conflicts arise; addresses problems and conflicts immediately and follows through to ensure that they have been resolved; and demonstrates consistency in management style, in the way he or she treats employees, and in his or her moods.

Discrimination can have legal consequences. Hiring standards and employee policies to prevent illegal and unfair practices must be established. Additional state and local laws may work with federal regulations or independently—some local laws contain provisions not included under federal laws. Good record-keeping practices that prove law compliance often enables managers to avoid penalties.

References

1. *Supervision in the Hospitality Industry, Third Edition* by Jack E. Miller, FMP, Mary Porter, and Karen Eich Drummond, FMP ©1998 John Wiley and Sons, Inc.

Learning Objectives

You will be asked to:

☆ Select an appropriate response for managers when employees communicate concerns.

☆ State what a foodservice operator should always do when communicating by letter with a customer.

☆ Determine who receives communication regarding an organization's mission statement.

☆ Distinguish between a strategic planning goal and an operational planning goal.

☆ Explain an effective strategy for implementing an operational change.

☆ Describe how a manager should deal with resistance from workers regarding impending changes.

☆ Specify how managers should begin a time-management program.

☆ Recommend a course of action for a manager trying to organize her time better.

Leadership and Communication Skills

No organization can run efficiently without effective communication among all of its members. The foodservice manager is crucial in fostering openness and a climate of trust, and in ensuring that all staff members are kept informed.

Leadership Skills

With competition and personnel issues becoming increasingly challenging, foodservice managers must be in charge—they must be leaders. Leadership, the ability to influence others and their actions, is vital to any organization. Effective managers know their leadership style. Leadership style dictates how managers motivate their employees and influence their employees' work. Good leaders should become familiar with each worker's needs and adapt their management style accordingly.

Leadership also includes empowering employees. Empowerment is a process of giving employees authority to make many of their own decisions. They should be responsible not only for their jobs, but for making the entire organization work better.

Organizational Planning

Managers of large and small foodservice operations will ensure greater profits and potential for growth by managing and continually measuring operational goals. These goals should be spelled out clearly in a mission statement or similar document so that owners, investors, employees, and customers are aware of the organization's place in the market. Clear goals then lead to some form of management by objectives in which all managers and employees integrate their jobs with overall company goals.

Implementing organizational strategies usually requires change from managers and employees. Such change is inevitable. In any successful planning, resistance is a normal human reaction to change. Strategies should establish a positive, trusting climate for change by getting people involved and committed while overcoming any negative reactions.

Any change should be approached simultaneously on two fronts: the logical and the psychological. Logical aspects of change include the facts, forecasts, alternatives, and practical advantages of the situation. At the same time, the people involved must be considered so that they accept the change. Always communicate any changes as directly as possible to your staff.

Give those affected sufficient time to understand the change and the reasons for it so they can make their goals consistent and themselves ready for the change. Decide how their individual talents can best be employed to contribute to the change. Involve workers in the process to create enthusiasm. Make sure all employees are trained to deal with any changes that occur. Careful planning for change at the onset affects how employees accept the inevitable changes in the future.

To help measure an organization's goals against results, and to aid in managerial decision making, an effective information system must be in place. To keep managers constantly informed about business activities, data must be produced, sorted, organized, and converted into usable reports. This information will lead to the most highly researched and least risky financial decisions.

Decision Making

The ability to make sound decisions lies at the heart of most managerial functions. Recruiting, hiring, training, scheduling, and marketing activities all depend on managers' decisions. Since decision-making is so pervasive, foodservice supervisors often juggle several decisions at the same time—hundreds on an average day.

A decision is a workable response to a situation or problem. A good decision is one that satisfies a reasonable number of people or adequately addresses a problem. While effective decision-making depends largely on a manager's leadership style and intuitive judgment, it is helpful to think of decision-making in terms of levels.

First-level, or strategic, decisions are broad policy decisions critical to the success of the operation, as with the advertising approach or food standards. These decisions are usually made by the top management of a company or an independent owner, with input from employees with a particular expertise. Second-level, or operational, decisions are made within the broad guidelines of company policy, but they usually deal with the operational strategy for fulfilling goals. Operational decisions direct the organization's day-to-day tasks, including hiring, scheduling, training, and routine tasks, such as how many portions to produce or the type of soap to buy. Performance, or third-level, decisions are the everyday choices made by all employees in carrying out routine tasks, such as deciding how to mop the floor or when to remove the french fries from the oil. To make the best use of their time and skills, managers should concentrate on the first two decision-making levels and give employees responsibility and guidelines for making third-level decisions pertaining to their jobs.

Managing Time

Finding the time to plan, organize, and implement change, structure work time, and manage all the other important supervisory tasks involves making the best use of one's time. Successful managers can implement some form of total time management that encompasses personal, social, and work time. It can help people recognize what they can and cannot control, and provide direction for striking a balance that promotes optimum performance.

Using time effectively involves following a time management plan. First, the manager must sort out long- and short-range goals to accomplish. Goals should be specific, attainable, and measurable. Equally important is determining the steps to take to accomplish these goals. Determining goals leads to improved output through monitoring deadlines, timewasters, timesavers, and organizational activities, delegating more responsibilities, and training employees more thoroughly.

The final stage in time management is daily scheduling. Set aside a few minutes every day to go over activities for the next day. List priorities by marking 1, 2, or 3 next to each item, depending on its importance. First-priority items must be done immediately; second-priority items have less urgency; and third-priority activities can wait. If a first-priority item requires a block of time for completion, schedule it. Reserve about one hour each day for uncommitted time to handle any surprises or to help during peak periods. Unscheduled time allows managers to remain flexible while still adhering to high-priority activities. Scheduling priorities each day will allow managers to set new priorities, determine new short-range activities, and continue regular daily planning.

Communication Skills

Listening is crucial to effective communication. Yet it is one of the least developed communication skills. Research shows that most people listen only twenty-five percent as well as they could. Inefficient listening can cost an organization money in lost work time, missed information, deflated morale, reduced productivity, and strained relationships.

All managers have a responsibility to hear, attend to, and understand what their employees, customers, and supervisors say. Active listening requires interest, intellectual alertness, and good attention habits. Since communication is a two-way process, it requires listeners to accept half the burden. The critical task for the listener is to consider an entire message before passing judgement. Then the listener must interpret the information and send feedback so the sender knows the message was heard.

Managers who share responsibility in the communication process by practicing good listening skills show their involvement with the speaker by giving clear, meaningful feedback. Giving feedback is the best way to verify the message and to react to what is heard. Repeating what someone has just said to you minimizes errors due to misunderstandings.

However, if feedback also includes positive or negative behavior that is passed from the speaker to the listener and back again, the interchange is known as the circularity of behavior. For example, a restaurant supervisor sees a dishwasher break three cups and yells, "How could you be so stupid!" The dishwasher then responds to this hostile message, "Who are you calling stupid?" The supervisor counters with equal hostility in, "That was a dumb move." The dishwasher provides more hostile feedback and quits. Supervisors need to be aware of circular communications to prevent negative cycles from starting.

A large part of the communication process is determined by nonverbal behavior. Nonverbal stimuli are the silent messages that facilitate the accurate transfer of meaning. They include any of the expressions, gestures, voice qualities, or body movements that normally accompany a speaker's words. Together with verbal cues, nonverbal communication forms a total message. In most situations, nonverbal communication supports or substitutes for spoken language. Body language repeats, complements, accentuates, or regulates what the speaker says. For example, a nod of the head can either be a signal to continue or a gesture of agreement.

In other instances, nonverbal communication contradicts, or even negates, the intended meaning of the verbal message. Studies suggest that when nonverbal cues are inconsistent with accompanying verbal messages, the listener usually believes that the nonverbal cues reveal the true message. Supervisors who continually send incompatible verbal and nonverbal messages may cause feelings of tension and anxiety among their workers. The most effective use of nonverbal behaviors shows acceptance and respect for the other person.

Managers must communicate through formal letters to customers, vendors, service companies, government agencies, and a host of other business contacts. While much of a letter's success depends on the style and tone used by its author, following several generic rules of effective letter-writing will enhance the letter's effect. Letters should be written in standard, business-letter format on paper carrying an official letterhead, logo, or other identifying mark. (If none is available, the operation's name, address, and telephone number should be typed at the top of the letter.) The body of the letter should be clear, direct, and to the point.

Business letters of all types should be recognizable as a business letter, and communicate clearly and professionally. Managers are wise to remember that everything bearing the operation's name greatly influences the image—positively or negatively—of the operation.

Meaningful Meetings

Meetings are important communication tools. They are a sensible way to handle many kinds of discussions, problem-solving sessions, presentations, and general updates on the organization. Meetings coordinate and unify team members and serve as powerful business tools.

Begin the meeting on time. Welcome the group, bring participants up to date on the issue, state the purpose of the meeting clearly and concisely, and state the ending time. Stay on track. Follow the time limits set in the agenda. Manage the meeting process, not the people. Get ideas on the table. Initiate the discussion, establish a plan, and keep it moving. Asking stimulating, meaningful questions provides information, encourages interaction, and promotes team cooperation—three keys to meaningful meetings. If you do get hung up on one point, summarize what has already been said and move on. To make decisions, discuss the issue from all sides with input from everyone, and then vote. Involve all participants in the discussion.

Close decisively. Warn the group that the meeting is ending, field any final comments, and summarize conclusions. Determine the follow-up and give specific instructions for action. Announce when and how the minutes will be distributed. Tell the group when and how they will be informed of the results, and if there will be a follow-up meeting. End with a positive statement. Thank the group for their attendance and attention, and give them a motivational boost.

References

1. *Human Resources Management for the Hospitality Industry* by Mary L. Tanke, FMP ©1990 Delmar Publishers

2. *Supervision in the Hospitality Industry, Third Edition* by Jack E. Miller, FMP, Mary Porter, and Karen Eich Drummond, FMP ©1998 John Wiley and Sons, Inc.

Review Questions

The following questions are structured to draw from your experience and education as much as this manual's content. Some questions may also prompt review of a topic listed in the references at the end of each section.

Recruiting and Hiring

1. In a foodservice operation, a job analysis does which of the following?
    A. Identifies labor needs
    B. Lists tasks to be completed in a shift
    C. Recruits new employees
    D. Lists responsibilities of a job position

2. Which of the following lists the tasks and responsibilities required of employees filling a particular position?
    A. Mission statement
    B. Job description
    C. Job analysis
    D. Staffing guide

3. To be most effective, managers should look for potential employees
    A. continuously.
    B. around holidays.
    C. during peak or busy periods.
    D. when positions actually open up.

4. You determine that your wait staff must expand by 40 percent. You currently employ twenty servers. How many new servers will you hire?
    A. Four
    B. Six
    C. Eight
    D. Ten

5. In order to promote good employee relations, the first people managers should look to when filling a position above the entry level are among
    A. newspaper advertisement respondents.
    B. competing operations.
    C. off-the-street job applicants.
    D. current employees.

6. Under the equal employment opportunity laws, you can require servers to be
    A. experienced in food service.
    B. under thirty years old.
    C. unmarried.
    D. U.S. citizens.

7. Joe put the following advertisement in the local newspaper:
    Assistant Cooks wanted for a major pancake house restaurant. High school diploma required and some experience preferred. Must be willing to work weekends. Minorities encouraged to apply. Interested? Call Joe at 555-9876. (An Equal Opportunity Employer)
    What part of this advertisement shows evidence of possible discrimination?
    A. A high school diploma is required.
    B. Applicants with experience are preferred.
    C. Minorities are specifically encouraged to apply.
    D. Only applicants willing to work weekends will be considered.

8. Joe is preparing to interview applicants for the assistant cook positions. He calls the person whose application shows the most experience to invite her for an interview. When she answers the phone, Joe hears an infant crying in the background and notices that she has a speech impediment.

    A. Joe should invite her to interview, but he should ask her whether the child he heard crying was hers, so he will know whether absenteeism is likely to be a problem.

    B. Joe should not invite her for the interview because her speech impediment will likely interfere with her ability to communicate with the servers.

    C. Joe should invite her to interview, and not ask about the child, but he should introduce her to the servers to see whether they can understand her.

    D. Joe should invite her to interview and base his hiring decision on her relative qualifications and references only.

9. Professional hospitality associations and the Centers for Disease Control advise that to protect customers and employees from the AIDS virus, it is necessary for foodservice operations to

    A. not hire "high-risk" employees.

    B. have all foodhandlers tested regularly for the HIV antibody.

    C. use sanitary measures for communicable disease prevention.

    D. require all new hires to provide proof of their HIV-negative status.

10. The primary reason to call a job candidate's reference is to

    A. answer questions on the candidates application form.

    B. answer any questions the candidate did not answer.

    C. confirm information given by the candidate.

    D. provide personal information to elaborate on the candidate's information.

Orientation and Training

11. The primary goal of a new employee orientation program is to

    A. establish a system of discipline and rewards.

    B. establish a training plan and method for evaluating progress.

    C. communicate general information about the company and the position.

    D. assess the reaction of current employees to new employees.

12. Which of the following is the most appropriate to discuss during employee orientation?

    A. Equipment maintenance

    B. Absence and vacation policies

    C. The tasks of each employee

    D. Tasks to be completed the following day

13. During the orientation process, the most effective way to present organizational policies to new employees is to communicate them

    A. both orally and in writing.

    B. in an employee handbook.

    C. through the new employee's co-workers.

    D. in a monthly meeting with all employees.

14. All employee training must include some form of
    A. group discussion.
    B. instruction from a more experienced employee.
    C. written and oral testing.
    D. communication and feedback.

15. A manager has asked a head server to help train two more servers. This will be costly in the short run, but the training most likely will pay off because
    A. the new servers will deliver better service and influence profits.
    B. the new servers will be able to replace the head server.
    C. no formal evaluation process will be necessary after training is completed.
    D. the manager will no longer need to give the new servers feedback.

16. Training objectives should state
    A. shortcomings in employees' current performance.
    B. salary increases after training is completed.
    C. monetary bonuses for participating in the training.
    D. the performance or work behavior desired after training is completed.

17. Which of the following instructors is most likely to turn out competent workers?
    A. Susan likes to keep her students interest by including interesting but unnecessary anecdotes about the task they are learning.
    B. Henri treats each of his students equally.
    C. Morris hands out praise when a learner correctly performs even the smallest step of a task.
    D. Alice warns students who can't keep up that they might be let go.

18. Trainers need to be
    A. aggressive enough so that the trainee realizes the importance of training.
    B. patient and responsive enough to train people with different learning styles and needs.
    C. critical and outspoken about everything an employee does incorrectly.
    D. narrowly focused on the single method of training they have practiced and perfected.

19. Benefits of effective training include all of the following except
    A. lower employee turnover.
    B. increased productivity.
    C. higher rate of table turnover.
    D. increased sales.

20. In evaluating the effectiveness of a training program, a manager must, above all,
    A. analyze the costs and benefits of the program.
    B. observe changes in employee morale.
    C. gather employees together to ask their opinion of the program.
    D. conduct all training herself.

Shift Management and Scheduling Employees

21. Work schedules typically cover which two time spans?
    A. Daily and weekly
    B. Daily and monthly
    C. Weekly and monthly
    D. Weekly and fortnightly

22. Which of the following will help a manager predict how many employees will be needed at a particular time?

    A. Job analysis

    B. Staffing guide

    C. Mission statement

    D. Job description

23. Who normally prepares work schedules?

    A. Headwaiter or manager

    B. Maitre d'hotel or headwaiter

    C. Maitre d'hotel or manager

    D. Manager or front waiter

24. Which of the following internal statistics is most relevant to determining the number of front-of-the-house employees to schedule?

    A. Customers served per hour

    B. Analysis of menu item sales

    C. Number of meals served daily

    D. Total daily sales record

25. In arranging work schedules, when should shifts overlap and why?

    A. Shifts should overlap after the busiest times, so servers can tell their replacements what to avoid.

    B. Shifts should overlap at the busiest times, to allow calm and no-rush service.

    C. Shifts should overlap before busy periods, to allow staff to take breaks.

    D. Shifts should never overlap, because it is a waste of money.

26. If an operation estimates 120 guests for dinner, and the number of covers a server is expected to serve is twenty, the number of servers schedule is

    A. four

    B. six

    C. eight

    D. ten

27. Which of the following records would be most valuable in determining the number of servers and kitchen employees that should be scheduled during the day?

    A. Analysis of entree sales

    B. Customers served per hour

    C. Monthly food cost

    D. Monthly labor cost

28. The most effective way to ensure timely communication among shift supervisors is to

    A. instruct supervisors to communicate through memos.

    B. hold daily meetings of all shift supervisors.

    C. use a log to record incidents and status reports.

    D. provide a bulletin board for supervisors.

29. A split shift is a schedule in which

    A. workers' shifts overlap in order to have more people working during peak hours.

    B. employees work during peak hours such as lunch and dinner and are off during the slow hours in between.

    C. employees regularly split their duties, for example, when the servers help the busers during busy hours.

    D. the dinner crew stays to handle the breakfast service.

30. After completing an employee schedule, managers should

    A. post it in advance so that all employees are aware of their hours.

    B. circulate it among employees on the first day of the new work period.

    C. finalize it so that no future revisions are necessary.

    D. communicate it individually and privately to each employee.

31. The best way for managers to oversee employee schedules is to
    A. allow employees to switch schedules without intervention.
    B. enforce schedules as closely as possible.
    C. schedule positions, not employees.
    D. schedule managerial and supervisory employees but not hourly employees.

32. In smaller operations,
    A. available service personnel should always be divided into two shifts.
    B. the basis for the work schedule is meal times, not the operating hours of the restaurant.
    C. planning must be done farther in advance.
    D. schedule changes can often be handled individually by arrangements between staff members.

33. Which of the following need to be brought to the attention of the service staff before the mean period begins?
    A. Menu items not available
    B. Directions for clearing and setting tables
    C. Training new staff members
    D. Filling coffee cups

Employee Supervision and Development

34. The best programs for retaining good employees are organized around
    A. retraining needs.
    B. information from exit interviews.
    C. the reasons long-term employees stay.
    D. your organization's historical records on turnover.

35. Workforce team spirit grows best when decision making is
    A. shared among employees.
    B. left to hourly employees.
    C. separate from the day-to-day work experience to avoid conflict.
    D. done by management, so that team members know what is expected of them.

36. When managers delegate responsibility for a task to an employee, they must
    A. relinquish all responsibility for the outcome.
    B. not follow up until the task is completed.
    C. communicate clearly to the employee what is to be done.
    D. monitor each step the employee takes toward fulfilling the task.

37. Of the following, the best example of delegating responsibility is when a manager asks a(n)
    A. server to bus a table when it is very busy.
    B. busperson to fill in for a dishwasher.
    C. assistant manager to authorize overtime hours.
    D. prep cook to weigh all ingredients.

38. If a long-term employee's performance suddenly slips, you should meet with that employee to do which of the following?

    A. Fire the employee.

    B. Put the employee on probation.

    C. Identify the problem and reach a mutual solution to it.

    D. Inform the employee of the disciplinary steps you will now take.

39. If you notice that a worker has left the last two nights before post-closing cleanup is done, your best approach is to

    A. speak to the worker about it right away to find out the reason the worker is leaving early.

    B. wait a while until the worker a chance to change behavior.

    C. fire the worker at once as an example to other workers.

    D. question all of the other workers on closing shift before talking to the worker.

40. A common mistake made by supervisors in an evaluation interview is

    A. being critical and focusing on mistakes.

    B. having workers help set the improvement goals.

    C. encourage workers to rate themselves.

    D. allowing workers to comment on the evaluation.

41. Linda, a new manager who was hired three months ago, is conducting an annual appraisal interview with Alan. Based on her observations of Alan's productivity and attitude, she has given him an overall rating of "needs improvement." Alan is surprised and distressed by this rating because he has consistently received above average ratings in years past. He begins to protest Linda's evaluation of him, claiming that she does not realize his accomplishments and contributions during the first nine months of the year. If Alan is correct, how should Linda handle Alan's complaints?

    A. She should listen to his complaints and change his performance evaluation if there is sufficient evidence to justify doing so.

    B. She should listen to his complaints, but she should not consider changing his performance evaluation unless he files a grievance.

    C. She should not allow Alan to continue to vent his anger, rather she should interrupt and ask him whether he would like to have input on his improvement goals.

    D. She should have him complete a self appraisal and use it to negotiate new ratings for each performance standard with him.

42. Before firing an employee, a manager should first

    A. have the employee's co-workers talk to the employee.

    B. warn potential employers of his or her bad performance.

    C. tell the other employees.

    D. issue a warning to the employee.

Use the following information to answer questions 43–45.

Sally Jones, a dining room supervisor at a family restaurant, was asked to complete performance review forms on all of her employees. Unfortunately, the forms had not been used for more than two years and most of her current employees had never had a performance review. Sally used the forms anyway and set up times to meet with each of her employees to discuss them. John, the first employee Sally met with, seemed nervous about the meeting because he had been counseled twice in the past few months about his poor customer service. However, Sally had rated John's performance, as she had everyone else's, as satisfactory or better, to avoid anyone being unhappy with the evaluation. At the meeting, Sally asked John to sit down and she read the evaluation form to him. She then asked him if he had any questions or comments. John, who felt relieved by his satisfactory rating, said no, quickly signed the form, and left.

43. Did John receive an accurate evaluation from Sally?
   A. Yes, or he would not have signed the evaluation form.
   B. Yes, because he learned that his work was satisfactory.
   C. No, because the evaluation form was not accurately filled out and there was no discussion.
   D. No, because employees should never be given a satisfactory rating.

44. To get the most out of the performance review, Sally should have
   A. rated John's general performance as unsatisfactory.
   B. rated John as unsatisfactory in customer relations and set improvement goals with him.
   C. asked John to remain standing.
   D. met with several employees at once.

45. As a supervisor, it is Sally's job to
   A. encourage communication during evaluation interviews.
   B. take immediate control during the evaluation interview.
   C. compare John to other employees.
   D. rate her workers well so she looks good.

Sexual Harassment and Managing Diversity

46. Which of the following is an example of a stereotype?
   A. An operation promotes Cinco de Mayo to attract nearby Mexican-American customers.
   B. A manager hires only women to be servers.
   C. An operation hires many of its seasonal employees from a local, traditional Black university.
   D. A manager observes that Asian workers are very good with their hands.

47. Of the following possible differences among employees, which of these usually appears to have the most significant impact on diversity issues in the work place?
   A. Culture
   B. Income
   C. Education
   D. Work experience

Use the following information to answer questions 48 and 49.

Marlene works as a server in an elegant restaurant, and she has a good, professional rapport with many of the regular customers. Mr. Williams, a business owner who regularly holds business dinners and banquets at the restaurant, persistently asks Marlene to go out with him and comments on her physical features. Marlene has consistently told him that she is not interested in going out with him, and she has politely asked him to stop.

48. Is Mr. Williams's behavior a form of sexual harassment?

   A. Yes, it is an example of third-party sexual harassment.

   B. Yes, it is an example of environmental sexual harassment.

   C. No, his behavior is socially acceptable among men in the business world.

   D. No, although the behavior is inappropriate, it does not fit any of the definitions of sexual harassment.

49. As a manager, what should you do?

   A. Discuss the importance of Mr. Williams's business to the restaurant, and ask Marlene to ignore his advances.

   B. Nothing, a manager should not address harassment of employees by nonemployees unless the employee's safety is in danger.

   C. Inform Marlene that dealing with Mr. Williams is part of the job, but if she is seriously disturbed by his behavior, she can be trained for a different job in the restaurant.

   D. Inform Mr. Williams that his unsolicited advances and comments make some of the employees uncomfortable, and ask him to refrain from making such remarks.

50. Janet, a white middle-aged manager, is confronting Juan, a young Latino buser, about the quality of his work. When speaking with Juan, Janet notices that his eye contact is poor, he speaks softly, and he does not acknowledge her comments. Janet is bothered by Juan's response. Which of the following would be the most appropriate way for Janet to respond to Juan's behavior?

   A. She should speak more clearly and reposition herself to improve eye contact with Juan.

   B. She should try to mirror Juan's behaviors so that he feels more comfortable.

   C. She should accept Juan's behavior as a cultural difference and do nothing.

   D. She should explain to Juan that his behavior is impolite.

51. Which of the following behaviors would help build a trust climate among a culturally diverse workforce?

   A. Determine what went wrong and who did it.

   B. Be sarcastic, but cleverly.

   C. Be secretive and aloof.

   D. Maintain honesty as a standard not to be compromised.

52. Most employees in a multicultural workforce are attracted to work well with managers who seem to be able to understand things

   A. from only their point of view.

   B. from the employees' point of view.

   C. as the right way and the wrong way.

   D. as the new and best way.

53. If two people who differ in culture are to get along with one another and work together, they must

    A. recognize their similarities and their differences.

    B. realize the cultural diversity is a barrier to overcome.

    C. rely on simple solutions to the problems.

    D. control their own destinies.

Leadership and Communication Skills

54. Which of the following is the best example of a strategic planning goal?

    A. The cook will prepare 180 dinner specials on Tuesday.

    B. The dishwashing machine will be replaced with a larger model.

    C. Our annual advertising budgets will not exceed 5 percent of sales over the next five years.

    D. Two new servers will be trained next week.

55. Several procedures are going to be changing in the operation you manage. Which of the following is the best and most efficient way to communicate this information to your staff?

    A. Post a memo on the bulletin board.

    B. Hold a staff meeting.

    C. Talk with each employee individually.

    D. Have your department heads pass on the information.

56. The best strategy for a manager implementing an operational change is to

    A. implement the change before soliciting employee feedback.

    B. involve employees in the implementation process.

    C. communicate only with fixed-cost employees about the change.

    D. terminate employees who resist the change.

57. When managers make a major change in a procedure that will affect all employees, their best action is to

    A. ensure that all employees are trained to deal with the change.

    B. select two or three employees and train them to deal with the change.

    C. wait to see how employees adapt to the change before training them.

    D. insist that employees work with the new procedure before asking questions about it.

58. The best way for a manager to deal with resistance from workers regarding impending changes is to

    A. dismiss those employees who express resistance to the change.

    B. involve the employees in planning and carrying out the change.

    C. give one employee information about the change and ask him or her to pass it on.

    D. wait until the change has been made to answer questions from employees.

59. Managers should begin a time-management program by organizing

    A. their individual tasks and goals.

    B. each work station.

    C. department heads.

    D. long-term plans.

60. Which of these is good advice for a manager who is trying to manage her time better?

   A. Unless something is an emergency and has to be given higher priority, accomplish tasks in the order in which they come to you.

   B. Set aside regular periods of time without interruption for interviews, training, long-range projects, and making important decisions.

   C. Do not spend time trying to figure out long-term solutions to your time problems because you are just using precious time that you need to accomplish your tasks.

   D. Allow people to drop in to see you anytime they have a problem or just need to talk, so that you can help them solve their problems faster and they can get back to work.

61. When employees communicate their concerns to their managers, the manager should always try to respond with some form of

   A. delegation.

   B. feedback.

   C. authority.

   D. judgment.

62. Whenever an operator communicates with a customer through a letter, he or she should

   A. write the letter in longhand.

   B. retain a copy of the letter for thirty days.

   C. explain the operation's operating procedures.

   D. invite the customer to return to the operation.

Use the following information to answer questions 63 and 64.

Rick manages a restaurant. A week ago, one of the employees heard Rick and the owner talking about how to handle the slow business on weeknights. Since then, several rumors have been circulating, such as employees having their hours cut or being laid off. A few employees have tried to discuss their concerns with Rick, but he simply told them not to believe everything they hear and that he would make a general announcement soon. When he does, he calls and tells the employees that Monday through Thursday, the restaurant will be opening one hour later and closing one hour earlier. Many of the employees are concerned and angry and they all begin asking questions at once. Rick is frustrated and tells them that the decision is final, so they just have to deal with it.

63. How could Rick have avoided the negative reaction from his employees?

   A. He should have given the employees the facts earlier in the week and addressed each of the employee's concerns.

   B. He should have tried to persuade them that this is the best plan for all employees, not just the upper managers and the owner.

   C. He should have posted the new hours on the bulletin board, told the employees to be sure to check the bulletin board on the way out, and that he would answer questions tomorrow.

   D. He should have told them that they will certainly be able to make up for any lost revenue due to decreased hours by earning more in tips, because the restaurant will be busier during their shifts.

64. Could Rick have benefited from having his employees participate in this decision?

    A. Yes. Employees should be involved from the beginning to the end of every management decision.

    B. No. Hourly employees should not be involved in decisions that affect the profits of a restaurant.

    C. Yes. Employees will understand and accept changes more readily if they have participated in the decision-making process.

    D. No. There was only one logical solution to the problem anyway, so even if the employees had participated in the decision, the outcome would have been the same.

Answer Key

Recruiting and Hiring

1. A	6. A		
2. B	7. A		
3. A	8. D		
4. C	9. C		
5. D	10. D		

Orientation and Training

11. C	16. D
12. B	17. C
13. A	18. B
14. D	19. C
15. A	20. A

Shift Management and Scheduling Employees

21. C	28. C
22. B	29. B
23. A	30. A
24. A	31. B
25. B	32. D
26. B	33. A
27. B	

Employee Supervision and Development

34. C	40. A
35. A	41. A
36. C	42. D
37. C	43. C
38. C	44. B
39. A	45. A

Sexual Harassment and Cultural Diversity

46. D	50. C
47. A	51. D
48. A	52. B
49. D	53. A

Leadership and Communication Skills

54. C	60. B
55. B	61. B
56. B	62. D
57. A	63. A
58. B	64. C
59. A	

Chapter 4 Outline

I. **Cost Control**
- A. Control Techniques
- B. Controlling Food and Beverage Costs
  - 1. Figuring Costs
  - 2. Potential Savings
- C. Controlling Labor Costs
  - 1. Employee Turnover
  - 2. Labor Efficiency
  - 3. Quality and Quantity Standards
- D. Managing Other Costs
- E. Cost-Volume-Profit Analysis

II. **Foodservice Budgets**

III. **Accounting Principles**
- A. Cash Management
  - 1. Cash Register Management
  - 2. Reconciliation of Bank Accounts
- B. Basic Accounting Statements
  - 1. The Income Statement
  - 2. The Balance Sheet
  - 3. Statement of Owner's Equity

IV. **Review Questions**

Chapter 4
Unit Revenue and Cost Management

Learning Objectives

You will be asked to:

☆ Calculate the average number of customers based on given information.

☆ Figure the average dollar sale based on given information.

☆ Determine the cost percentage of a beverage.

☆ State a major disadvantage of reviewing operational costs only on a monthly basis.

☆ Calculate a monthly food cost percentage.

☆ Identify a fixed-cost employee.

☆ Choose a benefit of ongoing training.

☆ Recognize an item that is not a determinant of total labor costs.

☆ Choose a non-controllable determinant of labor cost.

☆ Determine the effect of variable costs during an increase in business volume.

☆ Identify an indirect cost.

☆ Choose a category of expense related to food and beverage operations.

☆ Calculate a breakeven point.

☆ Explain the method of justifying hours of operation.

A foodservice operator must have the ability to forecast revenues, estimate sales volumes, and establish prices. Cost control is the process by which managers attempt to regulate and guard against excessive costs. An ongoing process, effective cost control involves many facets of the foodservice operation, including purchasing, receiving, storing, issuing, and preparing food and beverages for sale. It also involves the scheduling of the employees who perform these functions.

Improper purchasing, inaccurate forecasting, poor inventory control, poor receiving procedures, failure to follow standardized recipes, lack of good selling and service, and improper menu item selection can cause undesirable food costs. To control food costs, one of the most important aspects of menu planning, managers must forecast sales of menu items, control portions, and deliberately select food items that meet cost and operation needs.

Cost Control
Control Techniques

The control techniques available to managers vary. Setting both long- and short-term goals is the first step a manager should take to establish control. A generalized, four-step process provides the foundation for developing control techniques.

1. **Establish standards and standard operating procedures.** An effective mission statement, clearly communicated service polices, production schedules, and standardized recipes provide a solid foundation for a cost control program.

2. **Train all employees to follow established procedures.** Poor job performance can be costly. Providing employees with a well-developed employee manual and conducting regular training sessions are among the practices that will reduce the risk of poor performance.

3. **Monitor performance and compare actual performance with standards.** Establish a positive performance evaluation program that praises employees for adhering to policies and meeting or exceeding standards consistently.

4. **Take appropriate action to correct deviations.** Policies that serve no practical purpose or are impossible to follow can lead to high employee turnover. Discipline employees as needed, but also review and revise policies as necessary.

Although, in theory, control procedures are implemented for maximum operating efficiency, managers must ensure that these procedures do not create unexpected or negative results. Unnecessary paperwork and red tape or controls of small details will often result in employee inefficiency and resentment which ultimately will affect service to the organization's customers. Establish controls proportionate to risks and make them as administratively efficient as possible.

Controlling Food and Beverage Costs

It is very useful for managers to determine the food cost and food cost percentage. The food cost can be determined by adding all requisitions from the storeroom to purchases for a given time. This number is then divided by the sales for the same period to find the food cost percentage. Every operation will have a different food cost percentage goal, but generally, a food cost percentage under 45 percent is considered desirable. The trick is to match the goal to the actual percentage.

Comparing costs with sales must be done regularly. Knowing costs enables a manager to evaluate operations on a daily, monthly, or quarterly basis. Many operations gather cost information daily and compare these costs with sales information to determine the daily cost percentage. Each cost percentage is compared to those from previous periods to determine how well costs are being controlled. In general, comparisons are made for specific days of the week—sales and costs of Friday

last week are compared to those for Friday this week. If the comparisons are not favorable, the manager must find out why, then take action to adjust costs so that a satisfactory proportion of cost to sales is achieved.

Figuring Costs

A monthly cost report involves listing current figures along with the previous month's figures under the categories of food and beverage sales, net cost of goods sold, and food cost percentage. Viewed together, monthly figures can help managers judge the effectiveness of current operations. Thus, goals for improving performance can be set.

All inventories must be maintained and controlled regularly. Whether an establishment employs a physical inventory system or a perpetual inventory system, counting and recording the number of each stock item by hand can reveal costly theft or mismanagement of purchasing, receiving, or issuing procedures. Auditing inventory by taking a monthly physical count is a standard practice for most businesses.

To calculate the cost of goods sold, first determine the ending inventory valuation by totaling the unit cost of each item remaining in inventory. Monthly food and beverage cost is determined by the following equation.

Opening inventory	Items on hand, first day of the month
+ Purchases	
Total available	Total value of all items available for sale
– Closing inventory	Items on hand, last day of the month
Cost of goods sold	Includes waste and pilferage

For example, assume that an operation began the month with $4,050 in its liquor and beverage inventory, ended the month with $3,890 in inventory, and had receipts totaling $11,380 in purchases. The beverage cost for the month is calculated as follows.

$4,050	Opening inventory
+ $11,380	Purchases
$15,430	
– $3,890	Closing inventory
$11,540	Monthly beverage cost

It is important to note that adjustments to the monthly cost, such as account transfers, bar transfers, promotion expenses, employee meals, and complimentary items be made.

Reviewing operating figures on a monthly basis has one major disadvantage. Suppose that an establishment's figures for one month revealed ineffective operations, and corrective measures were taken to eradicate problems. The effectiveness of that action cannot be evaluated until another month has passed. In the meantime, the establishment could be losing money every day.

To determine more timely figures, daily cost calculations can be made. For food, the two categories of directs (perishables immediately put to use) and stores (nonperishables charged to cost when they are issued from inventory) form the basic components of the daily food cost. Depending on an establishment's individual practices, additional figures, such as employee meals, must be taken into account.

With all the information at hand, it is possible to prepare a simple, yet timely, report on an operation's food costs on a given day. Constructed daily, these reports make it possible to judge the effectiveness of current operations. In addition, it is possible to evaluate and modify the causes of undesirable effects as they occur.

Potential Savings

Standard cost is the cost of goods or services that the management has identified, approved, and accepted. It is ideally what a food item should cost without taking into account spillage, waste, evaporation, or unplanned events, all of which are likely to occur in an establishment. Comparing actual and standard costs allows managers to monitor the success of an operation. When actual costs are compared to standard costs, the manager can get a clear picture of any inefficiency in the daily operation.

Known as potential savings, the differences between actual and standard costs reflect the variance between existing and desired operational

conditions. The causes of these differences include overproduction, overpurchasing, and failure to follow standard recipes. By obtaining these figures on a timely basis, evaluation of operations becomes possible, and corrective steps can be taken. In comparing actual and standard costs, two methods are generally used: 1) daily comparison, and 2) periodic comparison. Both methods include totaling the number of portions of each menu item served, figuring out how much those portions should cost, and determining how much those portions actually did cost. While making daily comparisons are incorporated into a manager's daily routine, periodic calculations can be accomplished by determining standard portion costs for a randomly selected test period. When compared to actual costs, the extent of potential savings can be determined. If the test period is a typical representation of operations, efficiency can be measured, and corrective steps can be taken to improve results in the next test period.

Differences between forecasted and actual volume should also be assessed. While some differences are to be expected, major differences could signal inefficiencies in operations; adherence to production procedures and standard portion sizes should then be evaluated. In addition, major differences could be the result of a faulty forecast, signaling the need for improved forecasting techniques.

A sales mix record is also helpful in controlling food and beverage costs. This record shows the amount of each menu item sold over a specific period of time, and can be done daily, weekly, or monthly. By studying past sales mix records, a manager can see if a drop in an item's popularity is seasonal, caused by production problems, or poor server sales techniques. Adjustments to the menu and to purchasing and production procedures can then be made. This record provides a basis for forecasting production schedules and for planning volume purchases.

Controlling Labor Costs

The cost of labor in foodservice establishments is considerable, ranging from 15 to 45 percent in most operations. Maintaining control over these costs is essential.

Many factors help determine labor costs. Weather conditions, for example, are out of the manager's control, while service can be governable. Other determinants include labor legislation, labor contracts, employee turnover, sales volume, location, equipment, layout, preparation, menu, and hours of operation.

Employee Turnover

A major concern in the foodservice industry is employee turnover. The industry-wide figure is 100 percent, with some establishments displaying figures as high as 300 percent. When these figures are compared with overall turnover rates in other industries, which are normally 10 and 20 percent, the importance of taking preventive measures is incalculable. To determine the employee turnover rate, divide the number of departing employees by the total number of employees in an operation. High turnover results in tremendous labor costs because managers must constantly fill vacant positions and train new employees. Assorted hidden costs, such as fees to advertise job vacancies and employment agency fees, may also be incurred.

To prevent high turnover, it is essential that employees receive ongoing training and that training is measured and linked to job performance. When appropriately trained, employees perform more effectively and experience greater job satisfaction. In turn, these trained employees satisfy both patrons and management, and increase sales volume.

Labor Efficiency

To maximize efficiency and control labor costs, management must first identify variable-cost employees and fixed-cost employees. Variable-cost employees, such as servers and kitchen workers, relate in number to business volume and are usually paid an hourly wage. As volume increases or decreases, the number of variable-cost employees changes accordingly. Fixed-cost employees, such as

managers and cashiers, have little relation in number to business volume and are almost always salaried. As volume increases or decreases, the number of fixed-cost employees remains fairly constant.

For maximum labor efficiency, employees' work should be organized. Three steps for work organization include:

1. **Establishing an operational plan.** In establishing an operational plan, a manager must possess a clear vision of the operation's nature. Both the product offered and the service presented must be evaluated. Various relationships that should exist among employees also must be considered. A functional organization chart can be devised to view these relationships. Positions are listed according to their function within the operation, and lines are used to indicate authority, responsibilities, and relationships between the positions.

2. **Preparing job descriptions.** Staffing needs or tasks must be placed into behavioral objectives, such as "Serve guests." The task must then state specifically how it is to be performed and how it is to be evaluated. Thus, the task "Serves guests" becomes "Serves all food and beverages to guests at tables within one hour using correct table service techniques as described in the (operation's) Table Service Handbook."

3. **Preparing an analysis of business volume.** Business volume analysis involves hourly and daily tallies of the number of tables served. Each of these can be accomplished in several ways, and the figures obtained help management forecast the number of employees needed to meet business volume.

Once the steps for work organization have been completed, and the projected business volume has been determined, a manager can schedule both variable-cost and fixed-cost employees. The projected business volume is important particularly in the scheduling of variable-cost employees. A manager must forecast total business volume on a daily basis and schedule variable-cost employees according to demand. Schedules for fixed-cost employees are fairly permanent, although reassessment might become necessary when major changes occur.

Other factors related to labor efficiency are equipment and layout. The kind of equipment an operation uses may do many of the same tasks as employees. For instance, a machine may slice beef quickly, while an employee slicing a roast manually may take some time. Also, within the work area, the layout of equipment must facilitate, rather than impede, employees' ability to perform their tasks.

Quality and Quantity Standards

Standards for controlling labor costs fall into the categories of quality standards and quantity standards. In the context of controlling labor, quality standards are established by evaluating the restaurant's image and the nature of its clientele. A privately owned, fine dining establishment may require a higher level of skill of its employees than a cafeteria-style franchisee. To establish quantity standards, a manager must determine the number of times a task must be performed within a given time period. One method, conducted in restaurants in which sales levels remain relatively constant, is a routine assessment of staffing. Relying upon recollection, managers determine whether staffing has been adequate. Any necessary adjustments are then made.

A second, and more reliable, method used to set quantity standards involves a test period, during which information is collected. Sales volume records and the number of tables served each day are analyzed. Records detail the number of persons on duty in each of the fixed- and variable-cost categories. Judgments are then made regarding the numbers of employees and the appropriate job performances. Charts can be prepared for the test period, and a table of employee requirements can be formulated. This table might reflect staff needs at various levels of business volume. Standard employee hours, or the number of employee work hours required in each job category to perform forecasted work, can be ascertained. Daily comparisons of forecasted and actual hours worked can be conducted, which allows managers to evaluate the overall efficiency of labor.

Direct	Responsibility of specific department, supervisor, or manager
Discretionary	Nonessential; at the discretion of managers
Fixed	Not affected by revenue (in the short run)
Indirect	Responsibility of general manager or management; not easily allocated to one area
Joint	Responsibility shared by two or more departments
Opportunity	Incurred when pursuing a change
Relevant	Directly affects a particular decision
Standard	Projected for a given level of sales or activity
Sunk	Already incurred or must be paid regardless of the outcome of decision-making process
Variable	Affected by revenue

Exhibit 4.1
Types of Foodservice Cost

Managing Other Costs

Many decisions involved in foodservice management depend on the answer to the question, "How much will it cost?" The answer becomes complicated when the many different types of costs involved in a business, each with its own set of characteristics, are considered. *(See Exhibit 4.1.)* Managers must be careful to allocate costs—both direct and indirect—according to a logical system before making decisions. Depreciation, maintenance, and other costs over time must be figured carefully to help in large-purchase decision making. Other decisions, such as off-season closing and method of lease payment, depend on accurate cost analysis.

Cost control alone will not guarantee profitability in an operation. Essential measures must be taken to ensure that all sales result in appropriate income to the business.

Cost-Volume-Profit Analysis

CVP (Cost-Volume-Profit) analysis breaks down cost information into fixed and variable cost information that managers can then use to project breakeven points and profits or losses at different projected levels of sales. Ideally, sales should meet or exceed both variable costs and fixed costs. A fixed expense is one that remains constant despite increases or decreases in sales volume. A variable cost is one that greatly increases as sales volume increases and decreases as sales volume decreases. If sales exceed all costs, the remainder is considered profit, while if the costs exceed the sales, then the establishment recognizes a loss for that period. This can be expressed as the following equation.

$$\text{Sales} = \text{Variable Cost} + \text{Fixed Cost} + \text{Profit (or} - \text{Loss)}$$

The breakeven point is that level of sales at which an organization neither makes nor loses money. The basic formula to calculate a breakeven point is as follows:

$$\text{Breakeven point in sales} = \frac{\text{Fixed cost}}{1 - (\text{Variable cost} \div \text{Total sales})}$$

For example, using the above formula, if an operation has fixed costs of $20,000, variable costs of $70,000, and total sales of $118,000, then the breakeven point at which sales would have to achieve would be $49,140.05.

$$\text{Breakeven point in sales} = \frac{20,000}{1 - (70,000 \div 118,000)}$$

$$\text{Breakeven point in sales} = \frac{20,000}{1 - (.593)}$$

$$49,140.05 = \frac{20,000}{.407}$$

The operation must generate $49,140.05 in sales before it begins to recognize a profit.

To determine how many customers the above establishment must serve to break even, first divide the total sales figure by the total number of guests served to find the average customer sale. In this example, 14,750 customers were served and the average customer sale was $8.00.

$$\frac{118,000}{14,750} = 8$$

Next, divide the fixed costs by the average customer sale less the variable cost percentage—the ratio of variable cost to revenue—multiplied by the average customer sale.

$$\frac{20,000}{8 - (.593 \times 8)} = \text{Breakeven point in customers served}$$

$$\frac{20,000}{8 - 4.744} = \text{Breakeven point in customers served}$$

$$\frac{20,000}{3.256} = 6,142.5 \text{ customers served}$$

As long as the average sale per guest remains relatively the same, the establishment must serve at least 6,143 customers before recognizing a profit.

The percentage difference between the total sales or revenue figure and the variable cost percentage is known as the *contribution margin*. The contribution margin is very valuable for projecting breakeven points and desired levels of profit. In the above example, the variable cost percentage is 59.32 percent, or .593 (70,000 ÷ 118,000). The contribution margin in the example above is 40.68 percent or .407.

$$\begin{array}{r} \$118,000 \\ - 70,000 \\ \hline \$48,000 \div 118,000 = 40.68\% \end{array}$$

Using the above situation as an example, if the organization in the example decides that they want to generate $40,000 in profit, what will they require in sales revenue to meet that objective? Using a variation of the formula above, you can easily determine the level of sales that will be required. Simply take the fixed costs that need to be covered ($20,000) plus the desired profit ($40,000) and divide this total ($60,000) by the contribution margin (.407, or approximately 40 percent) to arrive at the required sales volume of $147,420.

$$\frac{\text{Fixed costs} + \text{Desired profit}}{\text{Contribution margin}} = \text{Required sales volume}$$

$$\frac{60,000}{.407} = 147,420.15$$

A simplified financial statement shows this example in statement form:

Revenue	$147,420
Variable cost (59% of revenue)	$87,420
Fixed cost	$20,000
Total Cost	$107,420
Profit	$40,000

To determine the minimum sales point—the sales volume required to justify staying open for a given period of time—you must know your food cost percentage, minimum payroll cost for the period, and your variable cost percentage. If an operation's food cost percentage is 40 percent, its minimum labor cost to stay open is $150, and variable cost percentage is 30 percent, then the minimum sales point would be $500.00.

$$\frac{\text{Labor Cost}}{1 - (\text{Food cost \%} + \text{Variable \%})} = \text{Minimum Sales Point}$$

$$\frac{150}{1 - (.40 + .30)} = \text{Minimum Sales Point}$$

$$\frac{150}{.30} = 500$$

An understanding of the relationship between volume, fixed cost, variable cost and contribution margin is fundamental to any operation interested in controlling costs.

References

1. *Basic Food and Beverage Cost Control* by Jack E. Miller, FMP and David K. Hayes ©1994 John Wiley and Sons, Inc.

2. *Principles of Food, Beverage, and Labor Cost Controls, Sixth Edition* by Paul R. Dittmer and Gerald G. Griffin, FMP ©1999 John Wiley and Sons, Inc.

Learning Objectives

You will be asked to:

☆ Describe what is involved in developing a budget.

☆ Give specific information, calculate budgeted revenue.

☆ Calculate a projection for budgeted food costs.

☆ Explain how to adhere to an operating budget.

Foodservice Budgets

The process of managing a business consists of two basic elements: planning and control. The process of planning future business activity results in a formal statement called a budget. A budget, the most common method of controlling business activity, is a realistic expression of management's goals and objectives expressed in financial terms. There are several types of budgets. A capital budget is one that is prepared to project expenditures for long-term capital assets and improvement. An operating budget is a forecast of revenue and expenses. A fixed budget is based on a specific level of activity or revenue, while a flexible budget is based on several different levels of sales volume. *(See Exhibit 4.2.)*

No matter which type of budget is prepared, each time one is, a similar sequence of steps is followed. The managers involved in the budgeting process must first establish realistic goals and objectives regarding revenue and then project the estimated expenses, labor, and capital required to achieve those goals. Operating results from the prior period must be known as well as assumptions about the next period operations. Once management accepts it, the budget becomes a standard to compare and measure performance. As actual income, expenses, and profits or losses are recorded, it is crucial to compare the budgeted goals with the actual results and take action to correct deviations or problems. This series of budgeting steps should be followed for all budgets regardless of complexity.

The process is more difficult when preparing a budget for a new business. Instead of using past trends as a basis for the budget, a combination of known facts, comparable industry averages, and formulaic equations must be used to determine revenue and costs. Elements in an equation to project foodservice revenue include number of seats, estimated turnover, estimated average check, and number of days in the year the operation will be open.

```
                Jennifer's at the Pointe

Budgeted revenue per meal: $4.60

Staff meals budgeted:        1,300
Guest meals budgeted:       16,200
Total meals budgeted:       17,500

                         Amount   Percentage
Total budget revenue     $80,500  100.0%
Budgeted expenses
    Food                 $35,250   43.7
    Labor                $24,700   30.6
    Beverages            $11,600   14.4
    Total                $71,550   88.8
Income remaining          $8,950    1.11
```

Exhibit 4.2
Budget for Fourth Quarter

Although all types of budgets are important, it is usually the operating budget that receives the most attention. Basically the operating budget contains the forecast of revenue activity and the estimate of costs to be incurred in generating the forecasted level of profits. The operating plans of the managers form the basis for these budgets. While history and trends figure prominently in these plans, they should not necessarily be the sole basis for an operating budget, particularly in a situation where there are many new developments and factors to take into account.

References

1. *Basic Food and Beverage Cost Control* by Jack E. Miller, FMP and David K. Hayes ©1994 John Wiley and Sons, Inc.

Learning Objectives

You will be asked to:

☆ Calculate the closing balance in a restaurant's bank account.

☆ Identify an item that should be added to the balance shown by the bank when doing the reconciliation of a cash account.

☆ Determine whether a cash drawer is over or under at the end of a day.

☆ Calculate the amount of a cash deposit.

☆ Figure net cash receipts.

☆ Determine an operation's profit for a year based on given information.

☆ Choose the proper classification of a balance sheet item.

☆ Identify the basic balance sheet equation.

☆ Calculate a missing item from a balance sheet.

☆ Calculate retained earnings given certain information.

Accounting Principles

Information is crucial to the success of any business. Decisions involved in operations management, purchasing, personnel, and expansion all depend to a large degree on accounting and financial information. For instance, knowing past expenses and income is crucial to financial planning, purchasing, and hiring decisions. For financial information to be helpful, accounts must be kept in careful order and all transactions must be recorded accurately. Every foodservice manager will in some way be responsible for maintaining proper accounting practices.

Cash Management

The system that an operation uses to record sales and verify receipts must be efficient and understood by all employees. Where paper checks are used, they should be ordered by the manager only, kept in a secure location, and issued in recorded lots. The supply of checks should be audited to ensure that none are missing. However, more and more often, servers input customer orders directly into a computerized system. These systems often trace an order and automatically alert a manger of any discrepancies. Regardless of which system is used, every server must record sales and total each check completely and accurately. Product sales, guest check totals, sales receipts, and sales deposits should all amount to the same daily figure.

Proper cash management is one of a foodservice manager's most important responsibilities. To be effective, a cash management system must be accurate, secure, and service friendly. Two important aspects of cash management of immediate concern to the manager are on-site cash register maintenance and cash balance accounting.

Cash Register Management

Although there are now many sophisticated accounting systems and programs dealing with register management, a manager should understand the underlying principles and common cash handling practice. Fundamental cash drawer maintenance dictates that at the end of each business day a responsible employee must balance the recorded sales with cash and credit card slips in the cash register. Gross receipts minus change in the drawer at the beginning of the day should result in the correct actual receipts. In some establishments, this process may be done more than once a day. Similarly, bank deposits can be made more frequently to ensure that excessive amounts of cash are not at hand; however, service requirements for customers must receive high consideration. A foodservice operation must have sufficient cash on hand to cover change on large denomination currency and travelers checks.

Payment today is often made by credit card. Most credit cards are readily accepted with no identification because the bank or credit card company guarantees payment. However, the incidence of credit card fraud is very high. Make sure servers or cashiers always check the card for a valid date and get authorization from the credit card company. The guest must sign the credit card receipt; the name and signature must match those on the card.

In some establishments, disbursements are sometimes made out of the cash drawer. For control and security purposes, this practice is not a good idea. Receipt of cash and disbursements should be kept separate. Small amounts of cash can be kept in a separate Petty Cash fund for small incidental cash purchases and reimbursements, but most disbursements should be paid by check supported by the necessary authorization. Another safeguard that should be followed is separating the responsibilities for cash handling and cash accounting. The person who reconciles the bank accounts should not also handle the cash.

Reconciliation of Bank Accounts

An organization must maintain reasonable and accurate bank records in order to pay its obligations and reflect the true cash balance to its management and, possibly, other interested parties. It needs to reconcile its own records of cash on deposit with the bank statement to ensure that errors or oversights have not been committed by either the bank or the organization.

Reconciliation of accounts presents a problem for many people, but there are some simple rules to follow to ease the task:

1. Remember that you are trying to come to one agreed upon total.

2. Adjust the balance shown by the bank for items that you were aware of at the time the bank prepared the statement, but that the bank didn't know. Some common examples are:

    □   Deposits in transit, which are deposits you made that the bank had not yet recorded. This often happens at the end of the month. You need to add these amounts to the bank's balance.

    □   Outstanding checks, which are checks that have been issued but have not yet cleared the bank. You need to deduct these from what is shown as the bank's balance.

3. Adjust the balance shown in your cash account records for items that the bank knew, but that you didn't know. Some examples are:

    □   Unreported NSF checks: Not Sufficient Funds—i.e., "bounced checks." You need to adjust your cash balance downward accordingly.

    □   Bank service charges (deduct from your cash balance).

    □   Unreported collections on Notes Receivable held by the bank. You need to add to your account.

    □   Interest charges paid on your account— add to your account balance.

4. If the accounts still don't balance, check the bank statement first for errors or things like a check clearing for a different amount than your deposit shows. If this doesn't work, then check your own records for errors.

The following is a simple example of reconciling a bank statement using the above variables.

Acme Bar and Grill

Bank Reconciliation for July 2000

Balance per bank statement	$18,000
Adjustments:	
Deposit in transit	+ 3,000
Outstanding checks	− 7,000
Adjusted bank balance	$14,000
Balance per the organization's books	$15,000
Adjustments:	
NSF check	− $2,000
Bank service charges	− 300
Bank collection of note receivable	+ 1,200
Interest paid	+ 100
Adjusted cash balance per organization books	$14,000

Basic Accounting Statements

There are many types of financial statements, but the two that are of the most concern to the foodservice operating manager are the Income Statement and the Balance Sheet. There is a third that is of interest particularly to the owner-operator of a foodservice operation: Statement of Owners Equity.

The Income Statement

Of all the financial statements, the income statement normally receives the most attention. It reflects the income and expense activity of an organization over a specified period of time, typically monthly, quarterly or annually. It provides information first and foremost to the managers of an operation. Of course, it can (and in many cases, must) be given to owners, creditors, government agencies, and other concerned entities or individuals. *Exhibit 4.3* gives a sample Uniform Income Summary for a food service operation. There can be many organization-specific variations in the type of revenues, costs, and expenses accounted for, but the basic formulas stay the same. For example, a subsidized food service may have sales, but also derive a significant portion of its revenue from a grant or subsidy.

Summary Statement of Income
Name of Restaurant or Company
Description of Period Covered by Statement

	Schedule Numbers	Amounts	Percentages
Sales			
Food	D-1	$	
Beverage	D-2		
Total Sales			100%
Cost of Sales			
Food			
Beverage			
Total Cost of Sales			
Gross Profit			
Other Income			
Total Income	D-3		
Controllable Expenses			
Salaries and Wages	D-4		
Employee Benefits	D-5		
Direct Operating Expenses	D-6		
Music and Entertainment	D-7		
Marketing	D-8		
Energy and Utility Services	D-9		
Administration and General Expenses	D-10		
Repairs and Maintenance	D-11		
Total Controllable Expenses			
Income Before Occupancy Costs, Interest, Depreciation, Corporate Overhead, and Income Taxes			
Occupancy Costs	D-12		
Income Before Interest, Depreciation, Corporate Overhead, and Income Taxes			
Interest	D-12		
Depreciation	D-12		
Restaurant Profit			
Corporate Overhead	D-12		
Net Income Before Income Taxes			
Income Taxes			
Net Income		$	$

Exhibit 4.3
Uniform Summary Income Statement

Adapted from *Uniform System of Accounts for Restaurants, Sixth Edition* ©1990 by the National Restaurant Association.

Summary Statement of Income
Full-menu, Tableservice Restaurant with Food and Beverage Sales
Year Ended December 31, 2003

	Schedule Numbers	Amounts	Percentages
Sales			
Food	D-1	$ 1,017,000	73.75%
Beverage	D-2	362,000	26.25
Total Sales		1,379,000	100.00
Cost of Sales			
Food		428,250	42.11
Beverage		92,000	25.41
Total Cost of Sales		520,250	37.73
Gross Profit		858,750	62.27
Other Income		7,750	.56
Total Income	D-3	866,500	62.83
Controllable Expenses			
Salaries and Wages	D-4	354,500	25.72
Employee Benefits	D-5	59,750	4.33
Direct Operating Expenses	D-6	81,250	5.89
Music and Entertainment	D-7	14,250	1.03
Marketing	D-8	23,750	1.72
Energy and Utility Services	D-9	34,250	2.48
Administration and General Expenses	D-10	69,250	5.02
Repairs and Maintenance	D-11	23,750	1.72
Total Controllable Expenses		660,750	47.91
Income Before Occupancy Costs, Interest, Depreciation, Corporate Overhead, and Income Taxes		205,750	14.92
Occupancy Costs	D-12	73,700	5.34
Income Before Interest, Depreciation, Corporate Overhead, and Income Taxes		132,050	9.58
Interest	D-12	6,000	.43
Depreciation	D-12	34,600	2.51
Restaurant Profit		91,450	6.64
Corporate Overhead	D-12	20,685	1.50
Net Income Before Income Taxes		70,765	5.14
Income Taxes		18,920	1.33
Net Income		$ 51,845	3.81%
Retained earnings, beginning of year		37,200	
Retained earnings, end of year		$ 89,065	

Exhibit 4.3 continued
Uniform Summary Income Statement

Adapted from *Uniform System of Accounts for Restaurants, Sixth Edition* ©1990 by the National Restaurant Association.

The Balance Sheet

Unlike the income statement, which reflects income and expense activity over a period of time, the balance sheet shows the financial condition of a business in terms of its assets, liabilities, and owners equity as of one particular point in time. The basic balance sheet formula is:

Assets = Liabilities + Owner's Equity

Assets are things of value owned by a business. They can be current assets such as cash, inventory, short-term accounts receivable, or long-term assets such as buildings and equipment. Liabilities are debts the business is responsible for and can be of a short-term nature (e.g., current accounts payable to vendors, payroll owed to employees) or long-term (e.g., loans for equipment, mortgage on a building, long-term notes or bonds). Owner's equity is the value of the business's assets left after deducting liabilities. In other words, it reflects the owner's interest in the operation's assets.

The information contained in the balance sheet helps managers and stockholders understand important financial information: the restaurant's ability to pay its debts, what portion of profits has been retained, and if any risk is involved in future operations.

The Statement of Owner's Equity

The statement of owner's equity shows the change from period to period in the amount and composition of owner's equity. The term owners equity is used here to apply to a wide variety of enterprise types: corporations, partnerships, sole proprietorships, and, in some cases, institutions.

The simple basic formula for showing the change in equity is:

Beginning Owner's Equity consists of:

Paid-in Capital, such as common stock issued or other direct investment in the organization.

Retained earnings from prior periods which is the result of earnings less payouts of earnings to owners.

Changes to Owner's Equity during the period

Add: Additional Paid-in Capital during the period (e.g., issuance of common stock)

Add: Net Earnings during the period

Deduct: Payouts to owners during the period (e.g., dividends)

Ending Owner's Equity

References

1. *Basic Food and Beverage Cost Control* by Jack E. Miller, FMP and David K. Hayes ©1994 John Wiley and Sons, Inc.

2. *Management by Menu, Third Edition* by Lendal H. Kotschevar, FMP and Marcel R. Escoffier ©1994 The Educational Foundation of the National Restaurant Association

Review Questions

The following questions are structured to draw from your experience and education as much as this manual's content. Some questions may also prompt review of a topic listed in the references at the end of each section.

Cost Control

1. Reviewing operating figures on a monthly basis has which major disadvantage?

   A. It takes another month to evaluate any corrections that are made.

   B. It repeats much of the information needlessly.

   C. It takes too much time.

   D. Month-old figures are often inaccurate.

2. To accurately cost a recipe using the computer, the foodservice manager enters

   A. current prices paid for goods, the recipe, and the number of times the recipe is made.

   B. the recipe and cost of ingredients.

   C. recipe and number of servings.

   D. current prices of ingredients, cost of labor, and number of servings.

3. A quick-service operation's cost of goods sold for the month was $21,677 and the average inventory value was $4,569. How many times did inventory turn over?

   A. 4.7 times

   B. 10.9 times

   C. 28.5 times

   D. 31.9 times

4. An operation's opening inventory for November was $4,320 and its closing inventory was $3,980. Food purchases for the month totaled $17,640. What was the cost of food sold?

   A. $17,980

   B. $19,240

   C. $22,480

   D. $25,940

5. Pouring-brand scotch costs $0.18 per ounce, and club soda cost $0.04 per ounce. How much does a scotch and soda calling for 2 ounces of scotch and 7 ounces of soda cost?

   A. $0.58

   B. $0.64

   C. $1.21

   D. $1.46

6. The scotch and soda in the above question sells for $3.75. What is its cost percentage?

   A. 17.1 percent

   B. 21.2 percent

   C. 34.6 percent

   D. 42.3 percent

7. A tavern had $9,438 in its liquor inventory on July 1 and $8,772 on July 31. Its July liquor purchases totaled $8,209. Its July sales totaled $36,440. Wine sales were $10,964. What was the tavern's cost of beverages consumed for July?

   A. $7,001

   B. $8,875

   C. $10,001

   D. $15,668

8. In a foodservice operation with a dining room, bar, and snack bar, which of the following would be an indirect cost?

   A. Alcohol

   B. Wages

   C. Food

   D. Building maintenance

9. A restaurant has estimated that its fixed costs next year will be $330,000 and its variable costs will be 34 percent of total revenue. At what level of revenue will the restaurant break even?

   A. $500,000

   B. $680,000

   C. $750,000

   D. $800,000

10. Which of the following is considered a direct operating expense related to food and beverage operations?

    A. China and silverware

    B. Music and entertainment

    C. Marketing and promotions

    D. Employee payroll and benefits

11. An average dollar sale, or cover, is calculated by dividing total dollar sales by the number of

    A. food and beverage items sold.

    B. customers served.

    C. servers working.

    D. seats.

12. If a restaurant has average daily sales of $3,000, 200 seats, average cover of $10, and 15 servers, how many customers per day does it average?

    A. 300

    B. 250

    C. 200

    D. 150

13. A restaurant with 180 seats serves an average 920 customers each day. What is the average seat turnover rate?

    A. 3.6

    B. 5.1

    C. 7.9

    D. 9.2

14. Which of the following is normally a fixed-cost employee?

    A. Dishwasher

    B. Server

    C. Buser

    D. Manager

15. A quick-service operation employs 46 people and has lost 30 in the last year. What is the operation's employee turnover rate?

    A. 55 percent

    B. 59 percent

    C. 63 percent

    D. 65 percent

16. A restaurant has scheduled 5 servers to work on Tuesday. Each server will work 8 hours. If 240 guests are served, then how many guests are served per labor hour?

    A. 6

    B. 8

    C. 10

    D. 12

17. Which of the following is not a determinant of total labor costs?

    A. Training

    B. Use of outside services

    C. Job specification

    D. Equipment

18. Which of the following shows relationships among job positions?

    A. Mission Statement

    B. Organization Chart

    C. Market Study

    D. Feasibility Study

19. A server receives a base pay of $6.00 per hour for hours worked in a standard 40-hour work week. There is an overtime premium of 50 percent paid for overtime hours. The server normally works Monday through Friday. His timecard for the past week shows the following hours worked:

Monday	8
Tuesday	10
Wednesday	called in sick
Thursday	9
Friday	10
Saturday	6

    What was the server's overtime pay for the week?

    A. $9

    B. $15

    C. $27

    D. $45

20. As business volume increases, variable costs will

    A. increase.

    B. decrease.

    C. fluctuate.

    D. remain constant.

Foodservice Budgets

21. To evaluate the accuracy of labor forecasts, managers should conduct daily comparisons of actual hours worked and

    A. customers served.

    B. hours scheduled.

    C. seat turnover.

    D. variable costs.

22. Which of the following is a forecast of revenue and expenses?

    A. Capital budget

    B. Fixed budget

    C. Flexible budget

    D. Operating budget

23. A restaurant is preparing its annual budget for next year. Last January, monthly revenue was $44,620 from 2,748 customers. This year, the restaurant's goal is to increase check averages by 5 percent. If it achieves this and no other changes occur, which is the budgeted revenue for next January?

    A. $46,851

    B. $49,087

    C. $51,338

    D. $56,923

24. The manager of Real Texan Steak House spent $218,765 last year on food. She has added four new items to the menu and expects this to increase her food cost by 8 percent next year. If sales remain the same, how much should she budget for food costs?

    A. $138,512

    B. $184,555

    C. $236,266

    D. $281,558

25. If the manager in the previous question bases her budget on an estimated annual revenue of $788,900, what will be her budgeted food cost percentage?

    A. 30 percent

    B. 36 percent

    C. 42 percent

    D. 45 percent

26. A restaurant operator has paid $128,400 to a foodservice design consultant to redesign the facility. She expects her investment to translate into $250,000 in increased profits when the redesign is complete. What is the operator's expected return on investment?

    A. 19.5 percent

    B. 48.6 percent

    C. 167 percent

    D. 194.75 percent

Accounting Principles

27. This month, a restaurant had cash deposits totaling $19,400 and disbursements totaling $13,900. It started the month with an opening bank balance of $6,420. What is its closing balance?

    A. $10,900

    B. $11,920

    C. $12,900

    D. $13,280

28. When a monthly bank statement is reconciled to a company's records, what should be added to the bank statement?

    A. Deposits to the account not yet recorded by the bank

    B. Interest earned on deposits

    C. Outstanding checks

    D. Service charges

Use the following information to answer questions 29 and 30.

At the end of the day, a cashier's register tape shows net sales of $525, including charge sales of $50. Net cash in the drawer is $485.

29. Reconciliation indicates that the cash drawer is

    A. short $10.

    B. over $10.

    C. short $60.

    D. over $60.

30. Based on the figures and assuming that the bank collects the charge sales, the cashier's bank deposit for the day will be

    A. $415.

    B. $475.

    C. $525.

    D. $535.

31. At the beginning of the day, a restaurant has a starting cash bank of $500.00, and at the end of the day the total is $6,824.20. The tips included in the register are $1,320.00. What are the net cash receipts?

    A. $5,004.20

    B. $6,324.20

    C. $6,824.20

    D. $8,644.20

32. You are provided with the following information for Jane's Restaurant for the past year.

Revenue	$750,000
Long-term Equipment purchases	$100,000
Operating Costs and Expenses	$625,000
Long-term loans	$100,000
Dividends to Owners	$ 50,000

    What was the restaurant's profit for the year?

    A. Loss of $125,000
    B. Loss of $75,000
    C. Gain of $75,000
    D. Gain of $125,000

33. A cash register shows sales of $907.94. In the cash drawer are paid-out vouchers for $12.18 and cash totaling $594.74. Charge sales vouchers in the drawer should total

    A. $301.02.
    B. $310.20.
    C. $325.38.
    D. $1,514.86.

34. A long-term improvement made to a facility being leased for ten years is an example of what kind of balance sheet item?

    A. Long-term liability
    B. Current asset
    C. Long-term asset
    D. Paid-in capital

35. Which of the following equations correctly states the basic balance sheet equation?

    A. Current assets – Current liabilities = Working capital
    B. Long-term assets – Long-term liabilities = Retained earnings
    C. Assets – Liabilities = Retained earnings
    D. Assets – Liabilities = Owner's equity

36. Which of the following is used to show an operation's sales and expenses over a period of time?

    A. Balance sheet
    B. Income statement
    C. Statement of source and use of working capital
    D. Cost-of-goods-sold statement

37. The Big Burrito Restaurant Corporation had the following financial data for the past year.

Revenues	$ 800,000
Costs and Expenses	$ 600,000
Paid-in Capital	$ 300,000
Beginning Retained Earnings	$ 400,000
Dividends Paid	$ 100,000
Current Assets	$ 200,000

    What are the ending Retained earnings?

    A. $100,000
    B. $200,000
    C. $500,000
    D. $600,000

38. Which of the following is usually a direct department expense?

    A. Marketing
    B. Rent
    C. Energy
    D. Building maintenance

39. The Brook County Medical Center Foodservice Facility is a subsidized food operation. The county board must subsidize the facility to the extent that the facility does not show a loss on its Income statement for the year.

    The following is information from the Facility's books of account for the year.

Revenue from food sales	$ 1,500,000
Operating Costs and Expenses	$ 1,800,000
Accounts Payable to Vendors	$ 200,000
Cost of Building addition	$ 400,000

    How much subsidy is the county board obligated to pay?

    A. $300,000
    B. $500,000
    C. $700,000
    D. $900,000

40. The following data is taken from the closing balances of Bev's Steakhouse's books of account:

Retained Earnings	$ 125,000
Cash	$ 32,000
Accounts Receivable	$ 18,000
Other Current Assets	$ 112,000
Long term Assets	$ 125,000
Revenue	$ 800,000
Cost of Food	$ 300,000
Long-term Liabilities	$ 50,000

    The only missing item from the balance sheet is Short-Term Liabilities. What is the correct amount?

    A. $18,000
    B. $62,000
    C. $112,000
    D. $350,000

Answer Key

Cost Control		Foodservice Budgets		Accounting Principles	
1. A	11. B	21. B	24. C	27. B	34. D
2. B	12. A	22. D	25. A	28. A	35. D
3. A	13. B	23. A	26. D	29. B	36. B
4. A	14. D			30. B	37. D
5. B	15. D			31. A	38. A
6. A	16. A			32. A	39. B
7. B	17. A			33. A	40. C
8. D	18. B				
9. A	19. C				
10. D	20. A				

Chapter 5 Outline

I. **Marketing**
   A. Planning
   B. Market Research
   C. Market Segmentation

II. **Advertising**
   A. The Menu as Advertisement
   B. Sales Promotions
   C. Advertising Campaigns
   D. Positioning and Strategy

III. **Public Relations**

IV. **Review Questions**

Chapter 5
Marketing Management

Learning Objectives

You will be asked to:

☆ Determine the elements of the contemporary marketing mix.

☆ Identify the four elements of the traditional marketing mix.

☆ State what marketing involves in the foodservice industry.

☆ Specify a critical management responsibility related to marketing.

☆ Differentiate strategic from operational planning.

☆ Choose a mix of activities that result in the best marketing decisions.

☆ Identify sources of internal marketing information.

☆ Distinguish between types of market research.

☆ Determine how properly executed market segmentation can increase sales and profits.

☆ Select a key objective of market segmentation.

☆ Identify an appropriate segmentation category.

☆ Identify a target market group for a specialized menu.

☆ Explain how an operation should change to increase profits based on market information.

The foodservice industry has experienced tremendous growth in the past decade. This growth, which is likely to continue, has led to increased competition in all aspects of the industry and has made strong marketing strategies crucial for all foodservice operations. To run successful operations, foodservice managers must understand the functions of marketing and possess the necessary marketing skills, such as sales promotion, merchandising, and public relations, to recognize the changes in their customers' needs and overcome increased competition.

Marketing

Marketing aims to discover consumers' wants and needs and then to satisfy them. Marketing is a general term involving three continuous activities:

1. **Ascertaining the needs and wants of consumers.** The consumer should be the manager's first priority since a restaurant comes into contact with individual consumers on a daily basis.

2. **Creating a product-service mix that satisfies customers' needs and wants.** The product-service mix is all of the products and services offered by an operation, such as food, beverages, atmosphere, party facilities, and customer service.

3. **Promoting and selling the product-service mix to generate a profit level satisfactory to the organization's management and stockholders.** All operations are in business to at least break even on their investment; the vast majority of operations are looking to make a profit. Therefore, all managers are concerned with the financial well-being of an operation.

An effective manager understands all aspects of the marketing mix. The concept of the *marketing mix* is not new. Traditionally, it has been defined as encompassing four components: product, place, promotion, and price. However, in recent years a more contemporary marketing mix with specific application to the foodservice industry has been developed. The contemporary marketing mix is made up of three components:

☐ Product-service mix

☐ Presentation: the use of location, décor, theme, and other elements to make the operation's product-service mix more appealing to customers

☐ Communication: the ways in which an operation communicates to its customers through advertising, customer surveys, and other means

Although many foodservice managers may think that marketing and selling are the same activity, they are not. While *selling* aims to convince consumers of the quality and superiority of a product or service, *marketing* focuses on discovering and satisfying consumers' needs and wants. When a product is marketed in the proper manner, very little selling is needed because the consumer need already exists, and the product or service is merely being produced to satisfy the need.

Planning

Increased competition among foodservice operators has increased the need for aggressive marketing strategies. Since effective strategies start with planning, it is a key factor in the success of any foodservice organization. *Strategic planning* usually occurs at the corporate level of multi-unit organizations and chains. This involves the development of the marketing program for several units and the coordination of chain-wide marketing activities. Strategic planning also can involve the long-term goals and tactics of a large independent operation. *Operational planning* is undertaken by management at the individual unit level or by the owner/manager to direct ongoing activities and short-term goals.

Marketing planning is a multi-faceted process that involves an integrated set of activities. It involves

assessing the competition and their activities; developing marketing strategies, objectives, and short- and long-term plans; refining the marketing mix; and forecasting sales. An organization must establish both strategic and operational strategies based in part on market research and segmentation analysis. The organization must then be sure to properly position the product-service mix. Understanding consumer trends is an ongoing task that must be performed if an organization is to anticipate and stay current with consumer preferences.

Although planning can be time-consuming and demanding, it is essential to determine consumer preferences, implement foodservice changes effectively and smoothly, meet objectives, and make decisions. While no plan is a guarantee of success, the following steps can help keep a plan focused and on track.

1. Analyze information gathered through marketing research, including feasibility studies and surveys.

2. Assess the organization's strengths, weaknesses, opportunities, and threats in relation to the competition and consumer environment.

3. Establish organizational objectives.

4. Develop several marketing strategies.

5. Evaluate the advantages and disadvantages of each alternative.

6. Select the best strategy.

7. Develop specific action plans and an implementation schedule.

8. Implement the plan and monitor the results.

9. Evaluate the results against established performance criteria.

10. Evaluate feedback to revise and improve the plan.

Market Research

In order to make effective marketing decisions, management needs relevant information about the marketing environment in which the organization functions. Lack of accurate, reliable information can lead to costly mistakes and poor planning.

A market analysis is a study that examines whether consumer demand is high enough to warrant opening a new business. A feasibility analysis is a study of the potential demand for and economic feasibility of a business and includes a market analysis. It is most often conducted to evaluate the risk of investing money in a new foodservice facility. A feasibility study analyzes an area's traffic patterns and economic conditions, such as employment. It looks at the competition and gathers information to base sales projections. It looks at demographics and helps identify potential customers by occupation, income level, age, sex, and educational level. Information on spending habits for dining out is useful as well. A feasibility study should cover all areas essential to development and operating success.

A situation analysis relates to a business already in existence and studies marketing strengths, weaknesses, opportunities, and threats of that business. It considers the marketing environment, location and community, competition, market potential, service, and marketing positioning and planning.

Managers can obtain internal marketing information from sales figures, employees, and customers. Gathering external marketing information through market research is more costly and time-consuming. Market research information is based on probability sampling, in which the responses of a small sample are generalized to the larger population. Because the results are so important, the sample must be chosen carefully.

Survey questionnaires are valuable tools in market research because they provide significant information at a relatively low cost. Surveys are also versatile, since they can be conducted through direct mail, personal interviews, and telephone interviews. However, they must be carefully and thoughtfully designed. Survey designers must determine exactly what type of information is desired and tailor the

questions to that end. Surveys should ask a variety of open-ended questions, in which subjects respond with subjective opinions, as well as closed-ended questions, in which subjects select their responses from predetermined choices.

The information collected through market research is invaluable to foodservice planning. In the form of a marketing audit, research data can show the strengths and weaknesses of marketing strategies and practices. Audits should be conducted systematically and on a regular basis.

Market Segmentation

Segmentation, or breaking down the potential market into smaller, homogenous groups of like individuals, is done to better understand consumers and serve their needs more effectively. Commonly used segmentation variables include demographic, geographic, psychographic, behavioral, and benefit variables. Segmented groups can then be evaluated and targeted according to their size, measurability (in numbers as well as purchasing power), and accessibility through advertising and promotion.

In the past, hospitality marketing efforts were directed at traditional families and adults under forty. Recently, however, the importance of other groups—working women, people over fifty-five, and racially diverse people—has been recognized, and marketing efforts are being shifted to satisfy the demands of these groups.

To help evaluate potential market segments and determine the level of demand, forecasting methods are used. There are two major forecasting methods: qualitative and quantitative. The most common forecasting method involves basing expected future demand on past sales histories. Predicting the market demand for a new product-service mix is more complicated. Marketers must make certain assumptions about the expected number of customers, frequency of customer visits, average expenditure per customer, and likely competitive responses.

Surveys are used again to determine market potential. Consumers are surveyed about their past as well as their anticipated behavior. However, the reliability of these surveys is questionable; respondents do not always answer truthfully or may not be able to accurately predict their future consumer behavior. Test marketing is another commonly used method to predict market behavior. Within this method, the potential market demand of a product or service is determined by offering it on a limited basis within a small-scale test area.

Remaining competitive means responding to consumer needs and promoting those responses. For instance, to satisfy consumers' nutritional concerns, many operations have added and then promoted broiled and baked items to menus that formerly featured mainly fried items. Most prepare brewed decaffeinated coffee regularly. High-fiber and low-salt foods, once found only on health-food restaurant menus, have found their way even into the quick-service market. Restaurants that once offered only small bowls of lettuce and tomatoes have installed full salad bars. Some restaurants offer special menus, such as early-bird menus, which appeal to seniors. The public needs to be made aware that an operation is responding to their preferences.

To remain competitive, foodservice operations must continually develop and improve their products and services. Some companies are innovators—they are the first to introduce a new product in the market. Other companies wait until the success of a competitor's new product is well established before introducing similar products in their own operations. This is called "follow the leader" strategy.

The successful foodservice manager will be one who keeps up with consumer concerns and preferences, examines them carefully, and maintains flexibility. Of course, friendly, courteous service is always most effective in differentiating an operation from its competitors and maintaining a positive relationship with consumers.

References

1. *Hospitality and Travel Marketing, Second Edition* by Alastair M. Morrison ©1996 Delmar Publishers

2. *Hospitality Marketing Management, Second Edition* by Robert D. Reid ©1989 John Wiley and Sons, Inc.

Learning Objectives

You will be asked to:

☆ Choose an example of suggestive selling.

☆ State the objective of most foodservice promotional activities.

☆ Determine the primary advantage of point-of-purchase advertising.

☆ Identify a point-of-purchase situation.

☆ Outline different types of sales promotions.

☆ Develop a promotion based on market information.

☆ Select the primary advantage of including coupons in promotional advertising.

☆ Specify the proper role of certain types of merchandising materials.

☆ Recognize an important aspect of successful menu copywriting.

☆ Determine the best place for a particular restaurant to advertise, given certain facts.

☆ Identify the first step in the process of developing an advertising campaign.

☆ Recognize a type of informal, but effective advertising.

Advertising

Advertising is any paid form of communication. It is one form of promotional activity. Simply stated, all advertising is a form of promotion, but not all forms of promotion are advertising. Ideally, advertising should accomplish four goals:

☐ Inform consumers.

☐ Reinforce present consumers' good experiences.

☐ Induce first-time patronage.

☐ Generate repeat business and loyalty.

Achieving these short-term goals leads to a foodservice operation's ultimate goal—more customers and higher sales and profits, as well as other benefits, such as brand recognition and image enhancement.

The Menu as Advertisement

An establishment's menu is its best advertisement. Communicating and selling are the main functions of a successful menu. If the menu communicates accurately through design and layout as well as through copy, it can sell the items on it.

The design of a menu contributes greatly to its legibility and patron reaction. Menus should reflect the atmosphere and "feel" of the operation. The eye should be pleased with what it sees on the menu. The printing and coloring should blend in with the logo or trademark of the operation as well as with the type of establishment. A menu should be an invitation to a pleasing experience and should not promise too much. Patrons should clearly understand what they are to get and the price they are to pay for it.

A menu's wording and item arrangement should be such that the reader quickly understands what is offered. If foods are offered in groups, it should be clear what foods are included. Foods usually should be listed in the order in which they are eaten. Simplicity of a menu helps avoid clutter.

Making menu items stand out promotes readability and clarity. Headings and lines can be used to indicate separations and help draw attention to specific items. The first and last items in a column are seen first and best. This is the place to put menu items you want to sell. It is possible to lose items in the middle of a column, so items that management may be less interested in selling, but that have to be on the menu, might be placed here.

Sales Promotions

Sales promotion is a sales technique that offers consumers an extra incentive to take fast action, either to buy the product or to ask for further information. Promotional activities are intended to create interest in and quick demand for new products and services, encourage additional customer purchases, and attract new customers. Some strategies promote the operation by pushing the product-service mix through point-of-purchase displays, brochures and flyers, or advertisements. Others seek to pull customers in and stimulate their consumer behavior by offering free samples, special price reductions, coupons, and contests.

Personal selling, also known as suggestive selling, is one of the most essential means of promoting your operation. Suggestive selling means offering guests the full range of products and services available without offending them. For example, recommending a dessert on the menu or asking, "What kind of cocktail can I bring you?" will help servers promote menu items.

Point-of-purchase advertising, or P-O-P advertising, reminds the consumer at the restaurant about special offers and merchandise. Types of P-O-P advertising include table tents, banners, and special menus. The primary advantage of P-O-P advertising is that it influences customers already interested in spending their money. Many major suppliers or vendors have standard merchandising materials available at little or no expense. To determine the best display points, study the layout of your restaurant and position P-O-P materials in well-lit areas where customers can easily see them, but

avoid interfering with actual serving areas. Try to unify all P-O-P materials into one cohesive visual theme. And finally, rotate P-O-P materials at least once every month to maintain customer interest.

Sampling and coupons are two of the most popular sales promotion techniques. Sampling means giving away free samples of items to encourage sales or arrange in some way for people to try all or part of a service. Related to sampling is bundling, in which operations package menu items together and sell the package at a discounted price. Coupons stimulate customers to try new products or services, increase sales temporarily, and add excitement and appeal to media advertising.

Sales promotions should be used sparingly to retain their effectiveness. Unlike public relation or advertising campaigns, sales promotions should achieve short-term objectives. Such short-term objectives include:

- ☐ Getting customers to try a new service or menu item.

- ☐ Increasing off-peak sales.

- ☐ Increasing sales in periods that coincide with major events, vacations, or special occasions.

Sales promotion results are more immediate and short term than marketing and advertising results. Therefore, it is especially important to carefully monitor implementation of sales promotion results.

Advertising Campaigns

A campaign is the overall plan or strategy that guides the development of all forms of advertising. Campaign planning is initiated by considering the competitive situation, current and potential target markets, and market positioning. Generally, campaigns are organized geographically on a national, regional, or local level.

A written sales promotion and merchandising plan should be included in a campaign. There are ten basic procedures for preparing a campaign:

1. Establish objectives.

2. Choose between in-house or agency development.

3. Set a tentative budget.

4. Consider cooperative sales promotions.

5. Select sales promotion and merchandising techniques.

6. Select media for distributing sales promotions and merchandising.

7. Decide on timing of sales promotions and merchandising.

8. Pretest sales promotions and merchandising.

9. Prepare final plan and budget.

10. Measure and evaluate sales promotion and merchandising success.

As elements of an entire campaign, every sales promotion and merchandising activity should be based on a clear set of objectives. These objectives are usually more short term than campaign objectives and, like marketing objectives, should be target-market specific, results-oriented, quantitative, and time-specific.

When campaign objectives are further detailed into tasks, the costs of pursuing a given target market can be determined. Setting objectives for each target market that is important to your business is crucial toward ensuring that the investment in individual target markets is justified. Costs can then be compared to the revenues and profits generated, giving an indication of each target market's worth.

Campaign objectives also must be expressed in terms of desired results. Because objectives frequently result from a need to increase current volume, revenue, and market share levels, these provide a good basis for writing results and are an essential tool for managers as they control, measure, and evaluate the success of advertising campaigns. Market research techniques, including post-testing, should be used to determine whether objectives have been reached.

An increasing number of foodservice operations are hiring ad agencies to increase their advertising effectiveness. The costs involved are usually high, but the quality and scope of the campaign is generally comparable. Operators must weigh the balance of these aspects in relation to their marketing objectives, budget, and product-service mix.

Operators should beware of ignoring advertising until sales and volume are down. Spending exorbitant amounts as a cure to boost sales, or cutting existing advertising funds to save money, usually are ineffective. Rather than dealing with advertising sporadically, managers should plan their advertising activities and budgets carefully.

Positioning and Strategy

Positioning involves discovering a niche in the market that gives a product or service an individual image, distinguishing it from competitors. In addition, a carefully planned strategy is crucial for effective advertising. The strategy should include:

☐ Clear objectives.

☐ A targeted audience representing markets.

☐ The key consumer benefit that will attract consumers.

☐ A tone and format appropriate for the operation's image, product and service, and the audience.

The appropriate positioning of a product-service mix involves three areas:

1. **Establishing and measuring the consumer's perceived image of the operation.** Marketers establish and measure consumers' perceived image of the operation to discover whether it matches the intended image. If the two do not match, then managers must move to rectify this.

2. **Defining and packaging the operation's benefits.** Marketing managers must clearly present the benefits offered by their operation to consumers. These benefits are important because consumers evaluate a restaurant based on what it will offer them. Consumers then

choose the operation that comes nearest to satisfying their needs and wants.

3. **Differentiating the product-service mix.** Consumers must have a clear and positive perception of an operation's image for the product-service mix to be successful. A way to convince consumers of an operation's benefits is to differentiate products and services from the competition. This helps the operation establish a *unique selling proposition* (USP).

Since all forms of advertising are expensive, it is necessary to study what type of advertising will best reach the maximum number of potential customers at the lowest cost. Basic types of advertising include print ads in magazines and newspapers, radio and television broadcasts, outdoor billboards and signs, and direct mail methods such as sales letters, flyers, and brochures. Each type has its advantages and disadvantages. A newspaper ad may gain immediate exposure, but the life of the advertisement is short. Magazine ads may be read several times by several people, but may require a long lead time between the placement of the ad and its exposure. Television commercials offer extremely wide coverage but are very expensive to produce. Radio commercials reach a large audience, but lack visual appeal. Finally, outdoor signs and billboards are relatively inexpensive but may lack timeliness.

To decide on a type of advertising media that will best suit particular campaign needs, answer the following questions:

☐ Whom am I trying to reach?

☐ When can these customers be reached?

☐ Where do they live and work?

☐ What is the best way to reach them?

Two key points in advertising are consistency and frequency. For example, the same small ad that runs in a magazine every month will draw more sales than a large ad that is different every time it appears, and appears only once or twice. Recent statistics show that before an average consumer will buy a new product or service, he or she must be exposed to it nine or ten times.

References

1. *Hospitality and Travel Marketing, Second Edition* by Alastair M. Morrison ©1996 Delmar Publishers

2. *Hospitality Marketing Management, Second Edition* by Robert D. Reid ©1989 John Wiley and Sons, Inc.

3. *Management by Menu, Third Edition* by Lendal H. Kotschevar, FMP and Marcel R. Escoffier ©1994 The Educational Foundation of the National Restaurant Association

Learning Objectives

You will be asked to:

☆ Choose how an organization should handle negative publicity.

☆ Explain how public relations activities influence other promotional activities.

Public Relations

Public relations activities involve managing an operation's relationships with consumers, media, communities, governments, suppliers, employers, and all other public groups. Through news releases, public appearances by owners or executives, sponsorship of community events, charitable acts, and dozens of other activities, operations do much to form people's perceptions. Publicity is the non-paid form of promotion that is generated by an operation's public relations activities. It is the free distribution of information about ideas, products, or services.

The main function of public relations is to maintain a positive presence among the public. It is in any operation's best interest to maintain a continuing, positive relationship with individuals whom it has direct contact with (customers, employees) as well as those groups whom it deals with indirectly (the media, the general public). Public relations also enhances the effectiveness of other promotional activities and advertising campaigns. It makes customers and the general public more receptive to the messages an establishment conveys and increases the likelihood that promotional techniques will be successful in achieving their objectives.

However, no matter how diligently an operation promotes its positive aspects to the public, it will encounter negative publicity at least once, if not many times, in its history. How you deal with negative publicity can have long-term or even fatal effects. When dealing with negative publicity, tell the truth and do not lie to the media. Do not try to cover up, for this will encourage the media to dig deeper. Gather all facts surrounding the incident and communicate them to the media. Dismiss rumors by stating facts correctly and completely. And finally, do not become defensive. Show a willingness to take action as a result of the incident.

It is much better for an organization to anticipate media requests for information and photographs than it is to scramble for them at the last minute. To provide accurate information to the media and public, foodservice operators should develop a press kit that includes the following:

☐ Fact sheet, with the operation's address, telephone number, number of seats, group facilities, and other information

☐ Description of the location and special or convenient features

☐ Special features of the establishment's products and services

☐ Photographs

☐ Biographical sketch of the owner or general manager

☐ Previous news releases, if still active or current *(See Exhibit 5.1.)*

References

1. *Hospitality and Travel Marketing, Second Edition* by Alastair M. Morrison ©1996 Delmar Publishers

2. *Hospitality Marketing Management, Second Edition* by Robert D. Reid ©1989 John Wiley and Sons, Inc.

[Print on your company's letterhead]

FOR IMMEDIATE RELEASE
[Insert month day, year]

CONTACT:
[Insert name]
[Telephone Number]

[Company's Name] DEMONSTRATES COMMITMENT TO FOOD SAFETY BY TRAINING STAFF

[Insert City, Date] – [Name of Company] is demonstrating a strong commitment to serving safe food by **[certifying [#] of employees; or planning to certify [#] of employees][give time frame]** in the National Restaurant Association Educational Foundation's ServSafe® food-safety training program.

Advancing food safety training for more than twenty-five years, the ServSafe program is recognized and accepted in more federal, state, and local jurisdictions than any other program. Through the program, participants learn important food-safety procedures, such as sanitation, time and temperature constraints, and HACCP (Hazard Analysis Critical Control Point) principles, which are essential in providing safe food to consumers. "**[Insert Restaurant]**'s food-safety training efforts show its customers and employees how seriously the company takes food safety, and that serving safe food is a priority," said A. Reed Hayes, President and COO of the National Restaurant Association Educational Foundation.

"As experts in food preparation and service, it is natural for us as restaurant **[owners or operators]** to take a leadership role in addressing the critical issue of food safety," said **[Company Executive or Owner]**. "We support the restaurant industry's position that the best way to help prevent foodborne illness is through food-safety training. By training our staff in the ServSafe program, we demonstrate our concern for our guests and our commitment to food safety."

In addition, each employee certified in the ServSafe food-safety training program is automatically eligible to participate in the International Food Safety Council, a coalition of all segments of the restaurant and foodservice industry that is dedicated to encouraging food-safety training within the industry. The Council also sponsors National Food Safety Education Month each September.

[You may want to insert your company name, along with a brief description of your operation, the number of units you operate, where they are located and how many employees you have, etc.]

The National Restaurant Association Educational Foundation develops, promotes, and provides educational and training solutions for the restaurant and hospitality industry. To find out more about the ServSafe program or any other Foundation training program, visit the Educational Foundation Web site at http://www.edfound.org.

Exhibit 5.1
Standard Press Release Form

Review Questions

The following questions are structured to draw from your experience and education as much as this manual's content. Some questions may also prompt review of a topic listed in the references at the end of each section.

Marketing

1. As it relates to the foodservice industry, marketing involves determining customers' needs and wants, creating the product-service mix that satisfies those needs and wants, and
    A. selling manufactured products to distributors.
    B. promoting and selling the product-service mix.
    C. purchasing a tangible product.
    D. identifying retail sales.

2. The traditional four elements—or four Ps—of the marketing mix include product, place, promotion, and
    A. people.
    B. production.
    C. price.
    D. presentation.

3. Which of the following activities is part of the marketing cycle?
    A. Creating a product service mix that meets customer wants
    B. Interviewing applicants for job openings
    C. Accurately tracking all business expenses
    D. Disciplining incompetent workers

4. The recent marketing mix, as it applies to the foodservice industry, includes production/service, presentation, and
    A. communication.
    B. place.
    C. promotion.
    D. price.

5. Management can obtain internal marketing information from sales figures, employees, and
    A. advertising agencies.
    B. trade journals.
    C. competitors.
    D. customers.

6. Which of the following characterizes the difference between strategic and operational planning?
    A. Operational planning is more time consuming.
    B. Operational planning is done by corporate managers.
    C. Strategic planning is done by corporate managers.
    D. Strategic planning is for the short term.

7. A critical responsibility of management is to instill the marketing concept in
    A. salaried employees.
    B. marketing employees.
    C. selected employees.
    D. all employees.

8. A potential business can evaluate its relationship to other businesses, property taxes, and zoning requirements using a

    A. market feasibility study.

    B. site evaluation.

    C. survey questionnaire.

    D. topographical study.

9. "We are going to attract more young, single people to our restaurant." This statement is an example of a marketing

    A. plan.

    B. method.

    C. goal.

    D. outcome.

10. The individual factors of life style, attitudes, and personality fall into which category of segmentation?

    A. Geographic

    B. Demographic

    C. Psychographic

    D. Benefit

11. From a market survey, you learn that the potential customers in your area are willing to pay average checks as follows:

    Breakfast $4

    Lunch $6

    Dinner $12

    This same survey leads you to believe that you can expect the following number of these customers, on average, for each of the three meals:

    Breakfast   200

    Lunch   250

    Dinner   150

Based on the above information, you should expect average daily sales of

    A. $4,700.

    B. $4,400.

    C. $4,100.

    D. $3,800.

12. Market segmentation is done to

    A. better understand consumers and market to them.

    B. evaluate past sales histories.

    C. position the product-service mix.

    D. differentiate products.

13. The first step in sampling is to

    A. design a survey.

    B. define a target population.

    C. design a marketing audit.

    D. calculate the return on investment.

14. When properly executed, market segmentation can increase sales and profits by

    A. cutting food costs.

    B. targeting the consumers most likely to patronize an operation.

    C. raising menu prices in an area.

    D. cutting down on advertising rates.

15. The Carraway Tearoom places brief but specifically worded questionnaires at each table in its dining room. Servers are trained to encourage guests to complete the questionnaires and return them to servers. This restaurant is using which type of marketing research?

    A. Observational method

    B. Random sampling method

    C. Experimental method

    D. Survey method

Advertising

16. To be successful, menu copy writing must
    A. be designed to sell the food items and their prices.
    B. list the food items and their prices.
    C. focus equal attention on all food items.
    D. not be concerned with the sequence of food items.

17. The primary objective of most foodservice promotional activities is to
    A. create employee acceptance and appreciation.
    B. foster cooperation with competitive businesses.
    C. increase consumer demand.
    D. keep production costs down.

18. Which of the following is an example of suggestive selling?
    A. Donating food to a church
    B. Sponsoring a local fund-raising event
    C. Recommending a dessert on the menu to a customer
    D. Putting an advertisement in a local magazine

19. The primary advantage of point-of-purchase advertising is that it
    A. influences customers who are already interested in spending their money.
    B. generally reaches a large mass audience.
    C. appeals to all segments of the target market.
    D. requires no employee training or extra spending.

20. Which of the following is an example of point-of-purchase advertising?
    A. Magazine advertisement
    B. Radio advertisement
    C. Table tent
    D. Billboard

21. A quick-service restaurant offers a hamburger, French fries, and a milkshake together for 15 percent less than what the items sell for separately. This technique is known as
    A. cross-promoting.
    B. merchandising.
    C. point-of-sale promoting.
    D. product bundling.

22. The primary advantage of including coupons in a promotional advertisement is that they
    A. distract customers when prices change.
    B. influence every customer who comes into the operation.
    C. are difficult to duplicate.
    D. provide a means to track the advertisement's exposure.

23. The primary role of merchandising materials, such as banners and table tents, is to
    A. introduce an operation's products to new customers.
    B. remind customers of what is available.
    C. create a need for new products.
    D. reinforce that customers have made good consumer decisions.

24. Brand recognition most often achieved through
    A. word of mouth.
    B. advertising.
    C. introduction of new products.
    D. special promotions.

25. When developing an advertising campaign, the first step in the process is always to
    A. determine the budget for the campaign.
    B. write the ad copy.
    C. determine the message of the ads.
    D. set objectives for the campaign.

26. Information about a service which travels from past to potential customers is knows as
    A. referrals.
    B. word-of-mouth advertising.
    C. the exchange process.
    D. evidence.

27. Late afternoon and "early-bird" menus can be most successfully directed toward which market group?
    A. Retirees
    B. Executives
    C. Families
    D. Working parents

28. Developing a service or marketing mix to occupy a specific place in the minds of customers is called
    A. location.
    B. segmentation.
    C. positioning.
    D. planning.

29. Gabrielle's, a French restaurant noted for its haute cuisine, is located in a densely populated, wealthy area of a large city. Which of the following is the best advertising medium for Gabrielle's?
    A. Billboard on a suburban highway
    B. Advertisement in a in a local college newspaper
    C. Advertisement in a city magazine serving the upper-middle class
    D. Advertisement on a local college radio station

Public Relations

30. A food service that donates its leftover food to charities or sponsors a Little League team is most likely to be making an effort toward
    A. good public relations.
    B. marketing the menu.
    C. merchandising food.
    D. looking for a tax deduction.

31. Publicity is often generated by sending what type of document to the appropriate contact person?
    A. Greeting card
    B. Press release
    C. Customer survey
    D. Annual report

32. How should an organization handle negative publicity?
    A. Cover up.
    B. Take the offensive.
    C. Tell the truth.
    D. Set up a special committee to investigate the rumor or event.

Answer Key

Marketing

1. B
2. C
3. A
4. A
5. D
6. C
7. D
8. B

9. C
10. C
11. C
12. A
13. B
14. B
15. D

Advertising

16. A
17. C
18. C
19. A
20. C
21. D
22. D

23. B
24. B
25. D
26. B
27. A
28. C
29. C

Public Relations

30. A
31. B
32. C